KATJA MEIER

Across the Big Blue Sea

*Good Intentions and Hard Lessons in an Italian
Refugee Home*

First published by Ficari Publishing in 2017

First Edition

Cover design by Michelle Grant; michellegrant.com
Copy editing by Shirarose Wilensky; pagetwostrategies.com

This book was professionally typeset on Reedsy.
Find out more at reedsy.com

To the Nigerian, Gambian and Syrian women I met during their stays at Dogana's refugee home.

And to Sergio.

Author's Note

Although most events recorded in this memoir did indeed take place in a small hilltop town in the Tuscan hinterland, I have changed the real name and exact location of this town to protect the identities of the refugees, operators and locals I met during my work at its refugee home. For the same reason, I have altered people's names and distinguishing characteristics, with the exception of friends and family who agreed to the use of their first names.

Prologue

In the early hours of the last warm August night of 2014, I was sitting in our Dacia station wagon with my Italian partner, wearing a wig made from a pink tutu, our two preteen children—still wide awake at two in the morning—and five young women from southern Nigeria, all of them drunk to varying degrees. The *Odyssey* had been the theme of the costume party we had just attended—an apt one considering our African guests had crossed the Mediterranean Sea on a decrepit boat only a few weeks before.

Fola occupied the front seat next to Sergio, and I reached out from the middle row to squeeze an old shopping bag under her chin. At twenty-three, she was the oldest and most inebriated of our Nigerian passengers. Her four friends were still sober enough to yell at her, and so was Sergio. Or was he shouting at me for having gotten him into this situation in the first place? It was hard to tell in a seven-seater car filled beyond capacity with the rambunctious citizens of the world's two most vociferous nations.

"I'm sorry, mum," Fola said.

"It's okay, don't worry."

"Mum—"

"Fola, don't turn around. Look at the bag."

"The bag, look at the bag!" The voices in the Dacia had morphed into a sudden chorus to remind Fola of her most important task: to aim for the bag.

Her first outburst of projectile vomiting had hit my pashmina shawl towards midnight at the party. Friends had signaled from the dance floor until I realized that I had to intervene. Fola was tall and stout, and it wasn't easy to steer her to the deck chair near the pool. She crashed onto it and fell asleep right away. Sergio had refused to drive her up the hill to the refugee home, and I had drunk too much to do so myself. I left her in her alcohol-induced stupor and followed Earth, Wind & Fire's call to "groove tonight." Surrounded by inebriated Greek heroes and exuberant Olympian goddesses, I danced to two more tunes before I went back to wrap my pashmina shawl around Fola's shoulders. A cloud of humidity had enveloped the green valley and Sergio was worried she might catch a cold, or worse yet a *congestione*, a party-crashing ailment known only to Italians. When I touched her lightly, she leaned forward, opened her mouth and expelled a mass of half-digested pasta, birthday cake and local red wine. I studied the new pattern on my Indian shawl and understood why Sergio hadn't wanted to drive off with her right away. A youth spent partying in Tuscan village bars had taught him better.

I had used the pashmina as a headcloth in my costume's interpretation of Cassandra during the early hours of the party. Unlike the Trojan seer, I wasn't predicting the future that night but contemplating the near past and wondering how things had gotten out of hand so quickly. Had I been gifted with Cassandra's premonitory skills and sense of foreboding, I would have understood that this hilarious, surreal and exasperating Tuscan summer night already held—like a precisely chiseled miniature—every single component, force and dynamic that would play out on a large scale in the following ten months.

I

Summer

1

I met Fola, Joyce, Hope, Precious and Izogie on a July morning at the townhouse in Dogana. The five young women were between eighteen and twenty-three years old, and had been transferred to the refugee home in the small Tuscan hilltop town after a short stay at the emergency reception center in Sicily. The home was managed by a charity that was already in charge of a women's shelter in the Tuscan countryside. The townhouse in Dogana had originally been opened up as a second shelter for women and children who were escaping domestic violence, but in the meantime, two rooms had been prepared for asylum seekers. In spring, the prefecture had informed the municipalities of the Tuscan province it was governing that because of civil war in Syria and unrest in Libya, the number of people in need of assistance and housing was expected to grow enormously during the summer of 2014. From early June, families fleeing Syria were expected to take up the beds, but they never arrived. We learned later that the Syrians left Italy's emergency reception centers quickly and independently to avoid having to stay in the country. They boarded northbound trains instead, hoping to reach family or friends who had already managed to make their way up to Germany and Sweden, and to other central and northern European countries.

Fola was wearing my mother's silk nightdress when I met her for the first time. I had sorted out a lot of clothes for donation in spring, and Sergio had insisted that the lace-trimmed mother-daughter hand-me-down had to join the Red Cross bag. The moment I saw Fola wearing it, I was pleased I had agreed to let it go; the coral-red silk looked much better on her than it ever had on any member of my family. She descended the stairs looking like a darker and heavier version of Beyoncé on Grammy night, albeit a very detached and unapproachable one.

I had arrived at the house early on Sunday morning, and Anna was the only one up. She and her three teenage children had been living in the townhouse since Anna had left her violent husband a year before. I was supposed to help Nina, one of Anna's daughters, prepare for an English exam, but Anna couldn't wait to tell me that the Nigerian girls were a handful. I spent half the lesson listening to Anna and then Nina reporting the offensive behavior of the new houseguests. Only two nights after their arrival, the young Nigerian women already seemed to be at loggerheads with Anna and her children. I imagined the problem to be one of language and cultural differences. Anna's family had been living in the house for nearly a year, and they had had the space to themselves for most of that time. Having to suddenly share kitchen and common spaces with five more people must have felt like an invasion to them, especially since they were hardly able to communicate with the new inhabitants. I was sure I could help sort this out. I knew little about Africa, let alone Nigeria, but I had traveled widely in my twenties and as a Swiss living abroad, I had seen my share of cultural misinterpretations and translations gone awry. For a start, the two parties sharing the house needed to establish some common ground. Once they knew a bit more about each other, and the house rules and cleaning schedules were known and respected by everybody, living together would prove less of a conflict.

Fola walked through the living room, where I was teaching Nina. I got up and walked around the table to introduce myself. I knew it would be important for the young women to receive a warm welcome so that they could feel at home. I told her my name and asked for hers.

"Fola," she said, and walked on into the kitchen.

I stood in the middle of the room and watched my mother's nightdress disappear around the corner before I remembered to sit back down again.

"See what I mean?" my student asked.

I got up four more times during the lesson to greet the other Nigerian girls as they came downstairs in short intervals to get their breakfast in the kitchen. Just like Fola, each of them walked across the living room without saying hello. The girls seemed oblivious to the new presence in the house or, in any case, not in the least interested in who I was and what I was doing there on a Sunday morning. Their disinterest struck me as strange, but I took their reserve and indifference as a consequence of recent shock and trauma. Teresa, the manager of the charity, had told me the evening before that the Italian navy had saved the girls from one of the overcrowded boats we kept seeing on the news. I expected them to be distressed from a harrowing trip and their time in war-torn Libya, and from just about everything that might have happened to them since they had left Nigeria.

I finished the lesson a bit early and joined the young women in the kitchen to try again. I introduced myself properly and explained that I would be at the house a couple of times a week to assist Nina in her exam preparation. "Should you have any questions, just shoot away whenever I'm here and I'll be happy to help, okay?"

They didn't have any questions.

"And if there is anything I can do for you right now—just let me know."

There was nothing.

"Also, if there is anything you don't understand in the house, like the washing machine, or let's see... the coffeemaker?"

Izogie picked at her painted fingernails. Hope made a face I couldn't read.

The idea behind my little speech had been to make these five young women feel safe and welcome; the result was that I stood in front of them feeling uncomfortable and fake. I had expected to meet a group of worn-out survivors relieved to have found a temporary home and grateful to every person who offered a friendly word. But reality proved itself much more complex than my naïve assumptions. I scoured my brain for something nice and useful to say; I wanted to keep this conversation going, even if it didn't feel like one in the first place.

"Do you know where exactly you are in Italy? We could look at a map together."

"Are we in prison?" Izogie said.

"In prison?" It seemed I wasn't the only one making wrong assumptions. "Why in the world would you be in prison?"

Four of the young women had been locked up for months in a filthy and overcrowded house in Tripoli before being allowed on one of the boats. I would only learn this later.

"We've been in here for two days." Izogie's voice filled the whole kitchen. "We don't know whether we can go out. The Italian people don't talk to us."

"Of course you can go out!" I said, and realized that I wasn't a hundred percent sure. Was it okay for them to leave the house? Why did they think it wasn't?

I called Teresa. "Yes," she said, "obviously, they can go out."

6

"Everything's fine." I was happy to be the bearer of good news. "You can go out."

"How do we get back in?" Hope asked.

"With the key," I said. The girls looked at me with raised eyebrows. "Don't you have a key?"

"No," the girls said simultaneously, and Izogie made a clicking noise with her tongue I had never heard before but would come to know well in the following months.

I was surprised to learn that the charity's staff had not left a key for the girls or taken the time to inform them about their exact whereabouts. I knew, however, that the social workers were having a challenging time at the main women's shelter in the countryside, which was full to the last bed with mothers and children who had all escaped extremely difficult situations. And to make things more complicated, Teresa had just been elected as a member of a Tuscan town council. While I was trying to chat up the five young Nigerian women residing at the refugee home, Teresa was spending Sunday morning repainting the local elementary school with a group of volunteers. Because of the country's stalling economy, the Italian education department and local town councils no longer had the money to pay for work like this. Also, the girls had not been left alone but with Anna and her family, who were supposed to give them a hand; it was just that they didn't know how to.

"So, now that you've discovered that I'm not a prison guard... is there anything you'd like to ask? Anything I can help with?"

"We need onions," Hope said.

"And pepper," Precious added. "There is no pepper."

"Okay, let me write that down so I remember to tell Teresa or somebody from the charity." I was relieved that at last there was a scrap of conversation underway. "And I will also make sure that you get a key."

"And where can we go? Do we have to stay in the village?"

I called Teresa again. "Where do they want to go?" she asked.

"I don't know. But I guess they'd like to know what they can and can't do." I knew they were not allowed to cross the border, but could asylum seekers move freely in Italy? I didn't have a clue whether they were allowed to travel from region to region, or even from province to province.

Teresa wasn't sure either. She had years of experience as the manager of the women's shelter, but she had never worked with refugees before. She promised to find out once they were finished with the painting.

Five minutes later, the house phone rang.

"You're looking for Izogie? Okay, hold on." I turned around to tell Izogie that there was a man on the phone asking for her. She took the receiver, started to talk in pidgin and disappeared into her bedroom on the upper floor. The other girls followed her before I could start a new conversation.

I spent some time going through the Red Cross bags scattered in the living room, wondering whether to stay or leave. Our kids were spending part of their summer holiday at my mother's in Switzerland, and Sergio was one of the volunteers who had grouchily sacrificed their Sunday to help Teresa repaint the school. I had promised to join them once I'd finished with Nina's English lesson but decided to hang out for a bit. I had always been better at sorting out social and relational mix-ups than at painting walls. Or was I? The rocky morning made me doubt the accuracy of my self-assessment.

I folded a few T-shirts and put them back in the bags. Nina had mentioned that the girls had hastily looked through everything, pulling out bits and pieces while complaining that they needed *new* clothes, not dresses and trousers that had already been worn by middle-aged European women. Perhaps clothes were a lot cheaper in Africa. Or were they just expecting Europeans to be so rich that they wouldn't ever bother with secondhand clothes? I folded an old jacket of mine and pulled out a black cardigan that had "Cashmere" written on its tag—something to take home if nobody else wanted it. I put it back in the bag for the moment and scribbled "shoes" on my pepper and onion note. Fola wore size 41. Finding nice used shoes in that size wasn't going to be an easy task among Italy's rather small-footed inhabitants.

"Did you talk to your family?" I asked Izogie, who had walked into the living room to put the portable phone back into the charger.

"No."

"No? Who was it on the phone, then?"

"Nobody."

"Nobody?"

"Just a friend."

"A friend who lives in Italy?"

"Yes."

"Good for you! You already have friends here. And what about your family? Have you been able to tell them that you've arrived safely?"

"I don't have family."

"You mean here or in Nigeria?"

"I don't have family."

"You don't have parents or siblings you'd like to call?"

Izogie clicked her tongue again.

"A cousin, an aunt?"

"No, nobody."

***

9

Two days later, I went back to the refugee home for another English lesson. I brought along two copies of the key. The girls had already started to explore the village, and Anna's family had opened the door for them when they wanted to get back in. Hope said that they were feeling a bit better now that they were able to go outside, and I was happy to hear that some intercultural cooperation was starting to take place at last.

"Did you like the town?" I asked.

"No," Hope said.

"No?" I was surprised and a little offended. There were much worse places in Europe than a Tuscan hilltop town. "Why not?"

"It's dead," Hope said. "There's nobody in the village. Only old people."

I thought of all the Tuscan pensioners sitting on benches in the sun. I kept flooding my social media accounts with photos of the well-groomed hat wearers. Obviously, a hip and trendy population didn't belong here, in the calm and unruffled life Tuscany was known for. I opened the French doors in the living room and asked Hope to join me on the terrace. Dogana sat on top of a hill overlooking a valley that was entirely covered with small vineyards and olive groves. A cypress tree could be made out here and there, just to ensure people didn't forget that this landscape had been shaped into perfection by generations of Tuscan farmers.

"The view is gorgeous, though, isn't it?"

"The view?" Hope laughed, and looked at me as if I wasn't quite right in the head. "All I see is bush."

"Right," I said, *But wrong*, I thought. True, there wasn't much going on, and these hills were an outback of sorts, but one that kept compelling a lot of foreigners to trade social security numbers, promising careers and safe pension plans for a life here. I thought that Sergio would get along well with Hope. My partner had grown up in this part of southern Tuscany and had always lived in the same village, just like his parents, and their parents and grandparents before. He appreciated his Tuscan countryside heritage, but he had yet to meet a foreigner who, unlike me, just saw these hills for what they were. Bush.

***

During my third visit to the house in Dogana, the atmosphere was less hostile, but conversations were still rudimentary. Answers were kept to a minimum, unless I really pressed. And they were mostly in pidgin which I hardly understood. I wasn't sure whether the girls answered like this on purpose. But even if not—it was obvious that I wasn't perceived as the friendly helper I wanted to be. If anything, I was an annoying presence bombarding them with unsolicited information ("Never throw your sanitary pads in the toilet."), too many questions ("How long were you in Libya and what exactly happened there?") and unwelcome requests ("Please, can you look up and say hello when I enter the room?"). Children were the topic that broke the ice on our fourth meeting. Mine. Not their presence or a photo of them, but hearing about their illegitimacy.

"Are you married?" Izogie asked.

"No," I answered.

"But you said you have two children?"

"Yes, a boy and a girl."

Izogie laughed and ran into the kitchen to tell Joyce. "This woman..."

I couldn't hear the rest of the sentence, only the explosion of cheerfulness it created—first in the kitchen and then up on the second floor, where the other girls were still in bed or in the shower.

"Born out of wedlock!" Izogie shouted when she came back into the living room with the rest of the group. Precious and Fola had towels wrapped around them, Hope was drying her wet hair and Joyce sat down on the sofa with a cup of tea in her hand.

"Mum, is this true?" Fola said. "You are not married?"

"No, I'm not."

"What about your kids?"

"What?" I asked. "What about them?"

Fola shrieked with glee. Joyce bent double with laughter and spilled her tea all over the sofa. I was surprised to see days of aloofness turned into gregarious hilarity by a concept that sounded very nineteenth century to me. I joined Joyce on the sofa, leaned back and took in the new vibe in the house, pleased that Sergio and I had never considered marriage. Hard to say what else could have produced such a good laugh and sudden crack in the ice as two kids born out of wedlock.

***

Later that day, Izogie and I had the first conversation that was not initiated by me.

"Mum, the Italians in the house, that woman, her children, they don't help us," she said.

"They're not here to help you. Anna ran away too. Her husband is crazy and violent. She moved here with her children because they need to hide. They will stay here until Anna finds a job and can afford to rent a place."

"They don't treat us nicely."

"They say exactly the same about you!"

Izogie laughed and shouted something I couldn't understand.

She was tough, the self-appointed gang leader, with broad shoulders and sharp features. I liked her right away. She dug into her plate of rice with chicken and offered me a forkful.

"So, her husband hit her?"

"Yes. I think so. And he must have threatened her and her children."

I tried the spicy rice and liked it. Izogie yelled something into the kitchen, and shortly after, Fola arrived with a plateful for me. The absence of good global cuisine was a recurring lament in Italy's expat circles. Since the eighties, there had been the odd Chinese restaurant serving microwaved factory food, and in recent years, kebab stalls had started to replace a coffee bar here and there to my son's immense delight. But mostly, the pride, care and love Italians reserved for their own cuisine resulted in total disinterest in the food of other cultures. This insular attitude had led to a strange case of culinary racism in northern Tuscany, where the city of Lucca had passed a law that prohibited the opening of non-Italian restaurants in its famous historic town center. The only good thing to come of it was that with Big Macs being just as foreign to Italy as spring rolls and curry, McDonald's had been banned from Lucca's city center too. Considering the culinary void that couldn't be filled by pizza, pasta or any other Italian invention, I could already see myself spending many a free hour up at the refugee home if that raised my chances for a plate of home-cooked jollof rice for lunch.

Izogie got up, walked to the kitchen and came back with a refilled plate.

"Mum?"

"Yes?" The girls never used my first name, and I was getting used to being called mum. I learned later that this was the Nigerian way to respectfully address a woman from a senior generation, but hearing it continually had made me feel like I had from one day to the next received five grown-up foster daughters

"Is he Nigerian?" Izogie asked.

"Who?" I said, while scraping the last morsels of food from my plate.

"Anna's husband."

"No, Italian. Why?"

"Beating her up. Just like Nigerian men."

Some traditions and practices changed from country to country. Others were universal.

2

"Prostitutes?" was the first thing Sergio said when I told him about the young Nigerian women I had just met. Men, Italian men caught up in nasty stereotypes. And my man was one of them. I was furious. Surely these girls hadn't survived crossing a treacherous desert, a war-ridden country and a menacing sea just to supply Italy's roadsides with young flesh.

"They're running from Boko Haram."

Sergio wasn't convinced.

Because of the expansion of the Islamic extremist movement in northern Nigeria, thousands of civilians had been abducted, tortured, raped, killed. In April, the kidnapping of several hundred girls attending a secondary school in Chibok had shined a sad spotlight on the atrocities committed by Boko Haram. Following Michelle Obama's lead, I had retweeted #BringBackOurGirls several times that spring.

***

Tuscany had seen an unusually rainy summer that year. Tropical in some ways. All over Italy, the warm, wet weather led to poor grape harvests, and most of the region's olive crops were destroyed by pests that thrived on humidity. But the early August day on which I volunteered to take the five young women to the immigration office at police headquarters in the city was hot—the paralyzing heat that makes locals complain incessantly and tourists stick to their villa pool.

I picked the girls up at seven in the morning, surprised to see that they weren't wearing any of their new old summer dresses but the synthetic tracksuits and flip-flops that had been given to them at the reception center in Sicily, their first stop after reaching safety. The tracksuits were green or blue, and each one had "Referee" written on the chest. I wanted to suggest changing into something lighter for our first trip into the city, but there wasn't enough time. The appointment at the immigration office was at nine. The drive from Dogana would take more than an hour. And we were supposed to meet Teresa on the way and had to stop at a photo booth to take the pictures needed for their asylum requests.

***

I pulled back the curtain of the photo booth in front of the train station and showed the girls how to whirl the stool up and down and which buttons to press to get the photos right. They had left Nigeria without passports, and nobody in the group had ever possessed any kind of official document in their home country, in Libya or anywhere else. We were chatting and waiting next to the booth for the pictures to develop when an elderly man stopped on his way to the station and asked what national team they were playing for.

"Senegal?"

I had noted the friendly and interested looks from several passersby. I had not expected to receive so many of them in the company of five black women in flip-flops.

***

"Don't worry, dear, we'll find an Italian husband for you" were the first words the immigration officer said, while looking Fola up and down. The officer wasn't fooled into sudden respect by an old referee tracksuit.

"What is he saying, mum?" Fola asked.

"Ah, nothing. Don't worry," I said, fiddling with her photos and already regretting that I had agreed to translate during the interview.

The officer settled into a chair behind his computer to take down the details for Fola's asylum request. We had already prepared a statement for Fola. It explained that she was asking for asylum in Italy because of the civil war in Nigeria and indicated which route she had traveled to get to Italy. I had written everything down for her before she signed the statement. Hope, Joyce and Precious wrote their statements themselves, since they had had schooling to various degrees. Fola and Izogie couldn't write and read, but they were able to spell their names and sign for themselves.

The interview moved slowly. Fola was asked about her date and place of birth ("Say that again!"), mother tongue ("Sure that's a language?") and education and former profession ("None, of course! Why do we even bother to ask?"). A whole life had to be condensed into answers of maximum two words, since anything more overtaxed the immigration expert's erratic computer skills. Short even by Italian standards, the officer didn't make up for his stocky build with a quick mind or expansiveness of soul. His office was filled to the ceiling with stacks of interview printouts held together in brown paper folders—the United Nations' bottom strata, neatly assembled in a provincial office in the Italian outback. The names were written in red on top of each dossier. The effect was equalizing and unifying—whatever the nationality and identity hidden behind the names, once they landed on this slush pile, applicants would be churned out on the other side as asylum seekers.

The phone rang, and the officer tried to pull a folder from the bottom of one of the stacks with the phone squeezed between his shoulder and chin. I watched the wobbly document tower and thought of my home country, confident that Switzerland had conceived of an approach to the bureaucracy of immigration that didn't include long and complicated foreign names written with felt-tip pens on cardboard folders.

An hour later, after feeding the national database two keys at a time, and a lot of complaining about the task, the officer handed Fola the printout to sign. She bent down and put her hands in front of her mouth.

"What is it now?" The officer asked in his nasal voice. "Another one who doesn't know how to sign?"

I didn't answer and pushed Fola out of the room. We made it to the toilet just in time.

The officer looked uncomfortable when we got back. Ebola had been on the news for weeks, but Italy's government had reassured everybody that the situation was under control in the country. Fola, Hope, Precious, Izogie and Joyce had had initial health checks in Sicily, like all the people arriving on the boats crossing the Mediterranean. A more detailed exam followed upon their arrival in Tuscany. Transfer to the permanent refugee homes from the emergency reception centers was allowed only once all the boxes were ticked. This routine had been set up throughout Italy and was followed strictly.

"I don't want her in my office. She is obviously not feeling well. The prefecture has guaranteed that the people we're talking to are in perfect health."

I couldn't wait to get out of his office, but I didn't want to have to come back and start again. All we were missing was Fola's signature.

"Car sickness—she isn't used to curvy roads," I said, thinking that the nervousness produced by his shitty welcome and arrogant behavior during the interview hadn't helped either.

The officer wasn't convinced. I insisted that my kids always felt sick on the drive to the city. Cruising Tuscany's cypress-lined roads was fun during a laid-back holiday but not when pressed for time because of an early meeting at the police station or with kids in the car. I kept blabbering about emergency roadside stops until the officer rolled his eyes and let us back in to sign the statement.

Fola slowly put down letter after letter, trusting that the officer and I had properly translated and reported what she had been telling us. I walked to the waiting area with her while the officer called on the intercom for an assistant to help with the interviews. A young, smiling female police officer arrived who spoke a bit of English and greeted the girls in a friendly manner. We split up into two groups, Teresa and me translating for one each. The four remaining interviews were done quickly. The looming threat of a fatal infectious disease had turned the lethargic procedure into a speedy assembly line. I made a mental note to remember the tactic for the future, and at the end of the interviews, thanked the friendly police officer for her help.

I was halfway out the door when the immigration officer called me back.

"You're coming from one fine country."

"Switzerland?"

"Yes, the Swiss and their approach to this whole mess! Do you know how asylum requests are handled by your most efficient nation?"

I did not. I only ever had to deal with immigration practices when moving to Italy. But Switzerland knew its share about immigration; the majority of our highways and buildings had been built by Italians, after all.

"The Swiss don't mess around. Once an asylum request is denied," the officer pointed to Hope and Joyce, who were standing in the open door, "these people are sent straight home. No rubbish like here in Italy, where immigrants can lodge one appeal after the other until they find a judge who'll let them stay. You sort things out quickly and once you're done—you put them on a plane, and ciao!"

The officer's tiny eyes sparkled. He either truly admired my country or was pleased that he had managed to sink my Swiss pride. Bureaucratic sluggishness and labyrinthine paper work has driven people into despair since long before Kafka's time, but the other side of the coin—administrative proficiency executed by overzealous law-abiding officials—could be even worse.

***

"Are you taking us to the hospital now?" Hope asked.

"Yes, let's go."

I threw a wad of soiled tissues in the trash and got into the car. Izogie had thrown up too. Like Fola, she had not been well in the early morning, but throwing up hours after our ride to town made the car-sickness diagnosis implausible. The day before, Teresa and I had already told Precious that we'd take her to the hospital after the appointment at the police station. Precious had been complaining about headaches and general malaise since arriving at the refugee home, but the doctor who came to the small clinic in Dogana twice a week couldn't visit her until her documents were in order. Until then, we had to drive our guests to the emergency ward in the city.

I drove through the midday heat and told the girls that Teresa would join us later at the hospital. She had other legal matters to take care of for some of the mothers and children living at the women's shelter.

***

Hardly a seat was left in the waiting room adjacent to the emergency ward's reception desk. I told a stern middle-aged nurse that Precious hadn't been feeling well for a few days and that Izogie and Fola had been sick in the morning. The nurse turned to the girls and asked in broken English who was feeling ill.

"Me," said all five of them.

"All of you?" The nurse turned back to me with an unfriendly look. I wasn't sure whether she meant to scold me for not having looked after them properly or whether she was pissed off that I had brought in lots of extra work shortly before a public holiday. Nor did I know why they all insisted on seeing the doctor. Hope and Joyce had been well. Or at least as well as one could be only a couple of weeks after spending three uncertain days in the hot hull of a boat drifting on the Mediterranean.

The nurse filled in some forms and told us to follow her along a long corridor. After several turns, we arrived in a small space made up of two tiny separate rooms with two beds each. The nurse opened a drawer and pulled out five surgical masks.

"Tell them to wear these." She left and came back with a reclining hospital chair while I explained how to wear the masks.

"Why, mum?" Hope asked.

"Risk of infection," the nurse said.

There were no windows in either room. Joyce and Precious

switched off the light, lay down on the beds and went straight to sleep. Hope and Fola occupied the berths in the second room, and Izogie stretched out on the recliner. They were chatting in pidgin.

I went outside to call Teresa. She arrived half an hour later, and we talked to a male nurse who informed us about the standard procedure for patients in the quarantine rooms. They were having a busy day and he warned us that we'd have to wait. I hadn't expected anything else. Nobody who was right in the head went to an Italian emergency ward around August 15, when Ferragosto, Mary's assumption to heaven, signals the start of Italy's major holiday season. Businesses close down and most Italians—doctors and nurses included—celebrate with a cold drink on a deck chair at the beach.

But the church people I was dealing with stayed put in the hot city. Teresa had met with Don Vito, the priest who was one of the founders of the charity running the women's shelter in the countryside and the townhouse in Dogana. They had discussed the situation and decided to offer me a job looking after the refugee home in Dogana. With the ever-increasing arrivals in Sicily, more young women were expected to be transferred to the townhouse in autumn, and Teresa's new position as a local politician made her work more difficult. Shortly after the girls' arrival in Dogana, a newspaper had reported that the villagers were furious because they hadn't been informed about the launch of a refugee home in their town. Before it was turned into a women's shelter, the palazzo in Dogana's old town center had been run as a day hospice for the elderly. It had been painstakingly restored, but its remote location in a steep medieval town in the Tuscan outback didn't make it popular for people in need of day care. When Don Vito's charity stepped in, the locals didn't protest. Teresa's work was respected and the women's shelter in the countryside was a known entity by then. With all the news on Italian TV about women threatened and murdered each year by husbands or ex-husbands, nobody wanted to seem unkind. And the children of the women residing at the shelter helped to keep the tiny local schools open, which were always in danger of being closed down because of lack of pupils. Most of Dogana's inhabitants were happy to welcome mothers and their children fleeing domestic violence in Italy. But not all villagers liked the fact that the townhouse now also granted refuge to women escaping violence and dire living conditions in faraway countries.

"I'd love to do it!" I said.

Teresa smiled her exhausted social worker smile.

"I thought you would."

I had worked at the women's shelter before but just once a week to organize activities for the kids. A dance class for girls and boys in the first year (which had ended in a great party), and in the second, the creation of a vegetable garden, which had led to crazy strawberry and cherry tomato battles but very little harvest.

Teresa had to move on to one of her many appointments, but told me we'd settle the details of my contract as soon as I got back from my family holiday in Switzerland.

Izogie, Hope and Fola were still chatting when I got back into the room. I divided the *schiaccia*, the Tuscan flatbread Teresa had brought along, and told the girls that I had been asked to look after them when I was back from Switzerland.

"You're going to Switzerland?" Izogie asked.

"Yes, tomorrow. We'll have to leave at four in the morning to avoid the worst traffic. Ferragosto is a big holiday in Italy and the roads will be jammed since everybody wants to get out of the hot cities."

"Can I come with you?" Fola asked.

"You can't go to Switzerland. You need papers first," Hope answered on my behalf.

"I can hide in her suitcase!" Fola turned to me, making a puppy face. "Please, mum, can I come with you?"

"I thought you are feeling ill!"

"No, I feel much better now. No more vomiting, I promise!"

I imagined voluptuous Fola hiding under a blanket in the back of our Dacia among bottles of Brunello wine and containers filled with extra virgin olive oil from our family grove. Smuggling a few bottles of Italian wine over the border had become a common practice with Switzerland not being part of the European Union, but an illegal passenger was a different matter. I would be useless at smuggling anybody over the border, or—even worse—having to be that illegal passenger myself. I told Fola, Hope and Izogie about a Swiss friend who stayed with me, and then traveled back home on the night train from Florence. My friend was eight months pregnant at the time and not sleeping very well. Nobody got on the train in Bologna and she was relieved to have the compartment to herself. Having heard about thieves on night trains, she locked herself in and slept soundly all the way to Zurich. Before getting off the train, she turned around to check she hadn't left anything and noticed a leather jacket under the berth she had slept in. She bent down to pick it up but stared into two brown eyes instead. She had locked herself in with a stowaway who had spent the whole trip jammed into the narrow space beneath her berth.

"Let me try that!" Fola said.

"Have you ever been on a train?" I asked. "There's not much

space under the berth."

"Somebody can squash her in," Izogie said.

"Right, but she'll also need somebody pulling her out!" Hope said, and the girls and I broke into a fit of laughter imagining the scene. A nurse opened the door and looked disapprovingly at the suspected Ebola patients.

"How long will it take for a doctor to visit them?" I asked.

"Quite awhile," she said, and closed the door.

Izogie stood up from the recliner and told me to lie down and relax. I told her to stay and sat on the edge of Hope's bed.

"We can go to Switzerland together one day, once you all have your papers."

"How long will it take?" Hope asked.

"I don't know. The police officer said today that things have slowed down a lot because of all the arrivals from Libya. And the permit you'll get to start with is just valid for Italy."

"Mum, I want to go to London," Izogie said. "I like London."

"You won't be able to go to London, or anywhere else in Europe, until the commission in Florence has decided whether they accept your asylum request or not."

"Do you think they will accept it?"

"I don't know, but yes, I imagine they will, considering what's being done by Boko Haram. And you're Christians running from Islamic fundamentalism—that could help."

The nurse came back wearing a surgical mask and told the girls to pull up theirs. We woke up Precious and Joyce. The nurse took their temperature and prepared to draw blood from each one to run some tests. Fola shrieked when she saw the needle. The other girls laughed, while the nurse and I tried to tell Fola to hold still. A doctor arrived and asked for a surgical mask before entering the room. The surgical masks made me

25

laugh, since I still hadn't been given one. At least I sacrificed myself for a good cause. The doctor asked me to translate a few questions and left after hearing the answers. Precious and Joyce joined us in our small room, which was far too small for the number of people in it. The nurse cleaned up the equipment and told them to go back and lie down in the second room. They were back in ours as soon as she was out the door.

Joyce and Precious had slept for most of the afternoon and were hungry and feeling more vivacious. We talked about Nigeria. Hope was the only one from Rivers State, but she had moved to Benin City with her mother as a child. All the other girls had mentioned Edo State during the interview at the immigration office. I googled a map of Nigeria on my phone and showed it to Hope. She switched to satellite view and zoomed in on the building where she went to school.

"And look—this is where my mum lived."

"Where is she now?"

"I don't know." Hope closed the map.

I had asked them about their families several times. Joyce had mentioned a younger brother. Everybody else said they didn't have brothers and sisters. A fact that wouldn't have surprised me in Italy, but Nigeria surely still had a higher birth rate than the *bel paese*. Either the girls were not telling me the whole story or I had to update my internal hard drive. The pictures my brain freed up when it read or heard a combination of the words "Africa" and "family" were all populated by big groups of people. Expansive families living in straw huts. And half-naked mothers feeding their babies with countless children assembled around them. Big-eyed, beautiful children standing together and smiling at the camera. And flies. Lots of flies.

Hope's satellite view on my phone had shown a city that looked bigger and busier than Zurich and most of the ones I had ever lived in. I would have to do some reading up.

Izogie again offered me her recliner. I agreed this time and sat down while Izogie inspected my dress.

"Mum is wearing an expensive dress today!" she said to nobody in particular. Izogie had this way of talking straight into the room. I was never sure whether she was just thinking aloud or really wanted to start a conversation.

"I'm not one for posh labels," I said. I was wearing a green Kookaï dress that day. Not as cheap as the H&M clothes or hand-me-downs I normally wore—it was definitely the most expensive piece I had in my closet. Izogie had a good eye. We talked about fashion and from there hopped to music and celebrities. I didn't know most of the names they mentioned, but Hope found a Nigerian party music mix on YouTube. We discussed the outfits of the artists in the videos and laughed a lot, and I promised the girls that I would take them dancing one day. The hilarity died down after awhile, and the boredom of the hospital wait caught up with us again.

Hope wanted to lie down and handed the phone back to me. The browser showed Facebook's log-in site. I only ever accessed Facebook from my computer.

"Did you check Facebook before?"

"Yes, mum."

"You are on Facebook?"

"Yes," Hope stretched onto her bed and yawned, "it's very popular in Nigeria."

∗

At five o'clock, the nurse reappeared to tell me that I had to accompany the five women to radiology for chest X-rays. We had been waiting for the whole afternoon. At least there was some action now. We followed her instructions to reach the radiology ward, and one after another, they were called in for their scan. The radiologist talked through a microphone from the adjacent room and waited patiently each time until I had translated what they had to do. Referee jacket off; T-shirt off; yes, the bra too. Breathe in breathe out, X-ray taken. Bra, T-shirt and referee jacket back on.

A teenager with a broken leg was next. He looked the girls up and down and mouthed "Referees" to his mother, who tried hard not to stare at our unusual little group. Her son was wearing a navy blue tracksuit too.

The radiologist sent us back to the quarantine room. The doctor would look at the X-rays, but it would take awhile.

"We have to wait again?" Izogie said. "Mum, I want to go home."

"Me too," Precious added.

"We can't just walk off. You all said you needed to see a doctor. We may as well wait for the results now."

"Mum, in Nigeria, when you feel bad, you go to the pharmacy and they give you a pill. You take it and you feel better. That's it."

I checked my watch. Seven o'clock. Sergio would be home from work and wondering why I wasn't there packing my bags. I told Izogie to keep her voice down and be patient, and called Sergio.

"You are where?" he said.

"In the hospital. I took the girls after their appointment at the police station. They weren't feeling well..." I stopped before mentioning that Fola and Izogie had been sick in our car twenty-four hours before we had to travel in it to Switzerland.

28

"It's taking ages," I said instead.

"No wonder, we're close to Ferragosto. But you better—"

My phone beeped and Sergio was gone. Too much satellite viewing on Google Maps.

***

At eight o'clock, we were still waiting. The girls were hungry, and Fola, who had thrown up several times that morning, was starving. Nobody had eaten since six in the morning. I had finished most of the *schiaccia* on my own, since they didn't like it. I walked out to look for a doctor. What was happening? A nurse told me again that the doctor who had to look at the results was busy. There was nothing she could do; we had to wait. I asked whether I could get something for them to eat. She was sorry, but dinner had already been served. She suggested the snack machine in the waiting room. I had already tried that one, but my coins had been just enough for the Coke Precious had asked for and a bottle of water. The staff couldn't change banknotes.

Izogie stood in the door and disapprovingly clicked her tongue. The nurse shooed her back into the room.

***

The doctor arrived with the test results around ten o'clock.

"Tell them they can all go home, apart from... Let's see: Fola... Which one is Fola?"

"What does she have?" I asked after pointing out Fola.

"A chest infection. Possibly pneumonia. She needs to stay. The nurse will be back to draw blood for another test."

"Mum, no, not more blood," Fola said after my translation. "I feel weak. Look how weak I am. They already took too much blood."

"Fola, you have a chest infection. They need to do another blood test to figure out what medicine to prescribe to get you back on your feet."

"Mum, I wasn't so weak when I arrived here." Fola's big voice reverberated through the little room. "They take too much blood."

At the same time that I was trying to calm Fola down, the other girls were getting her worked up. They were teasing her, and Fola was getting more and more theatrical about her refusal to stay in the hospital or supply the Italian doctors with more of her blood.

An hour later, the nurse opened the door in the company of a grumpy-looking man pushing a wheelchair. The nurse asked for Precious.

"No, no, it's her, not me." Precious pointed to Fola. "She is the one who has to stay."

The nurse explained that she had been instructed to accompany Precious, who would have to stay in the infectious disease ward. Fola shrieked with relief and jumped for joy.

I accompanied the suddenly frightened-looking Precious and told the girls to wait.

The wheelchair pusher didn't look pleased about his new client.

"Where are they from?" he said when we entered the elevator.

"Nigeria. They have just arrived."

He didn't say anything else.

"They had a horrible trip. Locked up in the hull of a boat."

He stared straight ahead.

"They're running from terrorism. And they are Christians too."

I felt like a clown pulling rabbits out of a hat to entertain a cantankerous kid's birthday party. Why was I trying to court an unfriendly hospital worker? None of my chatter would change his mind if he was one of the reactionary supporters of the extreme right. Nevertheless, I tried to gain points for the girls by insinuating that they weren't that different from him. When really, thankfully, they were.

Two nurses received us at the ward on the sixth floor. They showed Precious her big and empty room. I asked for a phone charger and one of the nurses told me to check in the bottom drawer at the reception desk. Patients always left them behind. A friendly but tired-looking doctor came by and told me that Precious had malaria. Untreated, probably for a long time. She wanted me to tell Precious that she might throw up from the malaria medication. And I had to ask her whether it was okay for them to do an AIDS test in the morning. This was customary practice with the blood tests, but patients had to give their consent. She nodded, looking frail and lost in the big room lit with fluorescent light. I wished there were another patient in the wide, empty bed next to hers. Sharing a room with another sick human being suddenly seemed a soothing option. Suffering was lonely enough in itself. I showed Precious how to switch on the light in the bathroom and which button to press to call the nurse. She lay down on the bed and looked terrified.

"I'll come back again later. I'm just going down to see which ward Fola will be in. I'll be back in half an hour or so. Okay?"

Precious didn't say anything and turned onto her other side. I had talked very little with Precious so far. Her aloofness had bewildered me from the first day. She was eighteen years old, but with her slender build, she could easily have been younger. Who could tell with no documents to prove it? Precious's skin was as black as skin could possibly be. She had the long limbs and regal posture of a ballet dancer and the high cheekbones of a model. I would learn later that she hoped to work as one, but this was unlikely to happen, as she wasn't tall enough. But a charity fighting hunger, AIDS or war in Africa would have cast her straightaway for the part of the beautiful native woman walking barefoot along a dirt road—all she needed was a colorful dress and a handmade basket to balance on her head. Fola or Izogie's much more robust frames wouldn't have fit the stereotypical images of starving people and snot-nosed children with flies in their faces that many NGOs still used to convince Westerners to donate for their causes. My generation had been raised with these well-trodden stereotypes, and working at the refugee home made me realize how many different versions of them were still lingering unquestioned in my psyche. But even worse, these clichés continued to form the minds of my own children. "Do Africans have phones?" my young daughter asked one day, genuinely surprised to hear that such elaborate technology existed on the continent she knew only from our TV screen. The programs had left her believing that Africans spent most of their time nursing baby lions and looking after injured elephants (unless they fought a war—at which point satellite phones came in handy—but the children's channels didn't go there yet).

I left Precious's room and overheard a nurse telling the wheelchair man that he could start getting the other girls.

"The other girls?" I asked.

"He has to bring them up one by one every half an hour. We've managed to find a bed for each of them on this ward."

"I thought the other ones were supposed to come back with me. Fola was the only one asked to stay, because of a chest infection."

The nurse looked at a notepad.

"They've asked us to prepare five beds. All of the patients are female and have foreign-sounding names. Are they all yours?"

I checked the names on her notepad, nodded and went back downstairs with the wheelchair man.

"I'll accompany you with each of them, okay? That way I can translate and they won't feel like they're left on their own."

"On their own? Five seems quite a lot!"

"I meant on their own in the middle of the night in a hospital in a foreign country. They all just had a terrible trip and risked their lives. I just want them to feel safe."

"They wanted to come here."

"Right," I said. There was no point in trying to explain. Especially not at one in the morning in an empty hospital elevator.

Fola had calmed down a bit. She was still nervous about more needles and drawn blood but felt reassured knowing that she wasn't the only one staying. Hope had a skin problem that needed checking, but I still didn't understand why Joyce and Izogie were being kept at the hospital. But I was too tired to wait for the doctor to come by once they had all settled into their beds on the ward.

I opened the door to Precious's room. She was facing the wall and her regular breathing sounded like she was sound asleep. I unplugged my phone and tiptoed back to the door.

"God bless you, mum."

I turned around to look at her. She was sitting up staring into the empty room. Her regal attitude had vanished. She looked like a worried and delicate child caught in an antiseptic and foreign world.

"You'll be fine, don't worry. The other girls are right next door, and Teresa will come by tomorrow to check on you."

I walked to the bed to squeeze her hand before switching off the light. I closed the door and felt sorry that I had to leave for Switzerland.

I put the phone charger on the counter of the reception desk and heard giggling from Hope and Izogie's room. I told them that Precious was in room 25 and asked them to check on her in the morning, before I walked along the green line towards the exit. I strode along a winding corridor lit with flickering fluorescent lights but couldn't find the door for the stairs. I followed the green line until I was back where I had started.

"Still here?" the nurse said without looking up, and pointed to a door behind her. "Take the elevator down. That will be quicker."

The big parking lot was completely empty at three in the morning, and I for once missed the vendors from sub-Saharan Africa who insisted on helping patients and visitors find a free parking spot. I normally paid them a euro or two for their help, hoping the tip would help me avoid having to buy anything, but normally ended up walking away with yet another set of cheap lighters, tissues or polyester socks. Not this time, though; parking the car in the company of five young Nigerian women had granted me the new privilege of not being asked to buy anything.

I started the engine, rolled the car windows down and drove out of the city. I had been up for nearly twenty hours but felt surprisingly awake. I was looking forward to my new job and to meeting our Nigerian guests properly when I was back from Switzerland. I cruised through the warm Tuscan summer night and felt the same lightness that I had often experienced during my first years in Italy. Encountering a new culture, and meeting people with a different mind-set and background, could be complicated and challenging—and extremely refreshing and rejuvenating.

3

I sat on a wooden bench in front of our Alpine hut and watched patches of eternal snow and zigzagged limestone change from yellow to orange to blood red. The Swiss mountain peaks were taking a glorious bath in the evening light. I put down the phone and opened a bottle of beer.

"The girls are fine," I said, and looked over to Sergio.

He didn't respond. He had fallen asleep in the hammock while I was on the phone with Teresa. Eleven years into our relationship, a child-friendly Alpine hike still managed to knock him out.

The girls were all back at the house. Izogie and Hope had left the hospital after two nights, Joyce and Fola after three, and Precious after four nights. It was good to know that they were well. I covered Sergio with a Swiss army blanket, kicked off my hiking boots and opened my laptop to google the hiking trail to the opposite side of the valley, where a narrow ridge called Schweizer Tor—the gate to Switzerland—connects two daunting limestone peaks that mark the border with Austria. The friends who owned the chalet had told us that the Schweizer Tor had indeed been a gate, albeit a tricky one to reach. Smugglers had used it for centuries, and during the Second World War, refugees arriving from Austria and beyond climbed up all the way to the ridge to descend into Switzerland on the other side in search of safety. It was an illegal border crossing point no longer in use, and from what I read in our

German-language guidebook, many of the refugees didn't make it across. They died of exhaustion or were sent back by the border guards who patrolled even remote areas like this. A few decades before the arrival of the refugees, Swiss children from the poor mountain valleys walked every spring in the opposite direction to farms in southern Germany to find work until the end of autumn, when they returned to their families before it started to snow. They were between six and sixteen years old and were auctioned to the highest bidder during child markets in Friedrichshafen and Ravensburg. The exploitation of children from destitute families in the Swiss and Austrian Alpine valleys lasted until 1921, when Germany's state of Württemberg decided that school attendance wasn't compulsory just for its own children but also for the ones from neighboring countries. Child markets—maybe I didn't want to hike up to these bloody mountain peaks after all.

I googled Nigeria instead and read up on its colonial history. I already knew that the British had orchestrated a totally arbitrary unification of various ethnic and religious groups. The Islamic north and Christian south had been merged into a frighteningly heterogeneous country. Flora Shaw, the wife of a British colonial administrator, had suggested Nigeria as the name for the newly created country. I read about the divide between the poorer north and the oil-rich south, which had been torn apart during the Biafran War. And about the ecological damage left by Shell and corrupt mismanagement. Benin City and Edo State were the names that I had managed to remember from the girls' asylum requests. It took two keywords (Edo State, emigration) to find the headline: "Trafficking in Women from Nigeria to Europe."

I took another sip of beer and clicked through to the website for the Migration Policy Institute. The article "Trafficking in

Women from Nigeria to Europe" was written in 2005 by Jørgen Carling, a researcher specializing in international migration. I read it once, and then went through it again, copying to my clipboard parts of the article with information relevant to the situation in Italy. It was depressing news.

Destination Italy

The most important European destination for Nigerian trafficking victims is Italy, where there may be as many as 10,000 Nigerian prostitutes. Other significant destinations include the Netherlands and Spain, and, to a lesser degree, Germany, Belgium, Austria, and the United Kingdom. Italy is the only European country where a clear majority of legally resident Nigerians are women.

The first Nigerian women who worked as prostitutes in Italy usually did so independently and were not trafficking victims. In the early 1990s, however, the rising difficulties of traveling to and settling in Europe meant that prospective emigrants were increasingly dependent on large loans.

Coupled with the prospect of large revenues on the Italian prostitution market, this provided an opportunity for traffickers. Young women were enticed with promises of good jobs, and subsequently coerced into prostitution in order to repay their debt.

The Emigration Pact

The victim's initial contact with the smugglers is often through a relative, friend, or other familiar person. After the initial contact, the victim is put in contact with a madam, the network's most important person in Nigeria. In many cases, the madam also has the role of sponsor, the person who finances the journey. Typical costs range from US$500 to US$2,000 for documents and US$8,000 to US$12,000 for the travel. The debt incurred by the victim is much higher, however. Typical amounts are between US$40,000 and US$100,000.

During overland journeys, men known as "trolleys" in the trafficking network escort women individually or in small groups. Nigerians play an important role in human smuggling in North Africa. The smuggling infrastructure that traffickers and their victims use also often serves asylum seekers.

In Italy, Nigerian sex workers are usually street prostitutes and constitute the low-wage end of the prostitution market. Their places of work (joints) are often located in the suburbs or along intercity highways. In the Netherlands and Belgium, Nigerian prostitutes are more likely to work in the big cities' red-light districts.

The trafficking of women to Europe is now a well-known phenomenon in Edo state. Many women therefore know they are likely to work as prostitutes if they agree to travel to Europe. However, they may have little understanding of the conditions under which they will work and of the size of the debt they will incur.

In anticipation of leaving Nigeria and helping one's family out of poverty, it is tempting for these women to believe in promises about good jobs. Whether this means being duped, or deceiving one's self, is not obvious. Importantly, the fact that the women may have known, or ought to have understood, that they would have to work as prostitutes does not excuse or legitimate subsequent abuse.

A Self-Reproducing Organization

It usually takes victims between one and three years to repay debts to their sponsors. The debt is sometimes increased as punishment, or the duration of the pact is protracted in other ways. Nevertheless, there eventually comes a day when the debt is repaid. The fact that the debt does not last forever may convince victims that adhering to the pact is their best option.

Once the pact has ended, it is common for a victim to work for a madam as a supervisor of other prostitutes, and eventually become a madam herself. In other words, Nigerian trafficking is not only characterized by female leadership, but also by a self-reproducing organizational structure.

Conclusion

Ironically, the strength of the Nigerian trafficking networks lies in the element of reciprocity between traffickers and victims. The religious and legal sanctioning of the pact between the two parties, as well as prospects for a better situation when the indentured prostitution ends, give the majority of victims a strong motivation to comply. As a result, Nigerian trafficking networks are less reliant on the use of violence than their Eastern European counterparts.

The victims' commitment to the pact makes it particularly difficult to combat this form of trafficking. In several European countries, authorities have "rescued" women from their traffickers, but they return to prostitution to fulfill their obligations towards their sponsors.

Fola, Precious and Joyce were from Benin City, the capital of Edo State—the hub not of terrorist attacks but of human trafficking. Izogie had grown up in the countryside and moved to Benin City as a teenager after her parents died. Hope was from Rivers State, but because of the oil fights shaking the region her mother had taken her to Edo State. I looked up from the screen; the limestone peaks were back to their usual gray. It had gotten cold, the Alpine iciness that cuts right to the bones once the sun is gone. I felt tired, my limbs heavy from the hike, the beer and the weight of the world. I tried a few other searches related to emigration from Benin City. All confirmed the information I found on the website of the Migration Policy Institute.

Sergio stirred and asked for a hand to get out of the hammock.

"I think you were right," I said once he was on his feet.

"About the hike?" He stretched his back. "Obviously. You're a nation of masochists. Only people totally incapable of kicking a ball could invent a sport like hiking."

The excellence of Switzerland's impeccably signposted mountain trails was eternally lost on him. But for once I preferred listening to his bizarre theories about Swiss outdoor life than to elaborate on what I had just read. We collected the bottles and plates of our aperitif to take them inside, and Sergio exploded in a fit of Tuscan swearing as soon as he crossed the threshold of our temporary home. The kids had left the door open and the chalet was teeming with flies, which hailed from the cows that were grazing right under its windows. Sergio set out to terminate some of them, while I got the fire going in the old kitchen stove. I loved the minimalism of Alpine life. No meal without a fire. Stirring the soup, I asked Sergio whether he thought this was exactly the kind of simplicity the Nigerian girls were running from.

"Your kids would," he said, pointing to the sofa bed.

Our daughter had fallen asleep over her Nintendo. Our son had run out of battery power and continued gaming on my smartphone. No trace of Heidi and Peter. I blamed it on their father, whose DNA must have messed up their otherwise immaculate Swiss gene pool.

We ate our soup and, in good mountaineering tradition, went to bed early after desperately trying to kill several dozen flies. Before falling asleep, I wondered whether people in Africa imagine Switzerland like this: majestic mountains, wooden cabins, solemn-looking cows and flies. Lots of flies.

***

Somebody is shouting in front of our window. I open the shutters and see a hunter in a green corduroy jacket and hunting hat with feathers waving to me from farther up the hill. He points to the other side of the valley. The night is pitch black, but the Schweizer Tor is lit up by an oversized floodlight, which sways from one side of the valley to the other.

"Jews!" the hunter shouts, then drops his binoculars and disappears. I pick them up and see a small group of people struggling to make their way down from the ridge. Somebody slips and falls into the darkness. I run into the valley and meet a small crowd of people at the bottom of it. The hunter is among them.

"Look at their feet," he says. They are barefoot.

A police officer escorts the refugees into a minibus, which I drive onto a Swiss highway in the middle of the night. The police officer sits next to me and smiles. "Don't worry, they can stay."

I slow down and look in the rearview mirror. A group of women is hidden under woollen blankets and their black faces are difficult to make out in the darkness. The police officer asks me to stop at the next service station. He gets out and tells the women to follow him. I start the engine, but before I drive away, I see that they are still barefoot. There is snow on the road; they need shoes. I call the police officer through the window and point to their feet. "You need to get them shoes!"

He smiles and says, "It's not worth it. They don't last that long. We used to give them shoes in the beginning, but they get killed or disappear, and the shoes with them. It's too big an investment."

"Why do they disappear?" I ask.

"These women just do," he says. "That's just the way it is, but don't worry, new ones always arrive."

I think he is a friendly man. He surely will look after them well. I look around, and the women are already gone. I shake the police officer's arm. "Look—the women, where are they?"

He smiles his friendly smile. "See, I told you so. It's a problem that resolves itself."

***

I woke up at two in the morning in a freezing chalet; Sergio had pulled away the blanket. I had a headache and a fly kept landing on my face.

4

I drove right to the refugee home on the first Monday morning after our holiday. Teresa opened the door, and I yelled, "Hi girls" up the stairs.

"Mum is back," somebody said on the upper floor, and Izogie, Precious, Fola, Joyce and Hope came down the stairs like an avalanche that swept me away in a turmoil of laughter and shouting. Izogie asked when I had gotten back, Hope wanted to know where my kids were, Joyce asked how the holiday had been, Precious said something in pidgin I couldn't understand and Fola just repeated, "Mum is back" while pulling the Swiss chocolate out of my bag. I had bought different types of Toblerone (milk, dark and white chocolate) depicting the Matterhorn mountain and two boxes of bite-sized chocolates in wrappers printed with views of snow-topped mountains and panoramas of the Swiss lakes.

I always felt better when I got back to Italy after a holiday in Switzerland. To feel alive and kicking, I needed things to be louder and more chaotic than in my sophisticated home country, which I missed for its efficiency and avoided for the lingering depression it triggered in me after a week or two. It was good to see the girls. I wanted to ask them how they were doing but had to surrender—it was impossible to make myself heard. I had learned since meeting them for the first time that Nigerians were upfront, feisty and unfriendly. And exuberant, fun and full of laughter, even in the grimmest circumstances. They were people of extremes, both good and bad, and I expected the girls to fit in smoothly in a country like Italy. Whether the behavior of five young women I had only known for a few weeks was representative of the deeper psyche of a multifaceted nation of 180 million, I did not know. But I was already infatuated with their forthrightness and sense of humor. It had to be expected—I have always had a weak spot for troublesome relationships.

Once the noise and excitement started to die down, I told the girls we'd be doing some Italian lessons later on, but I first needed to talk to Teresa, who was in the kitchen with Anna. Teresa had told me during my phone call from Switzerland that she had hired Lesley as a cultural mediator. Originally from southern Nigeria, Lesley had lived in Italy for more than a decade and had spent the last ten months living at the women's shelter. After years of violence and exploitation by her Italian husband, she had followed the advice of a women's charity to run off with her mum, Vera, and her three kids. The charity had found a place for all of them at the women's shelter in Dogana, and the children had started school in the village. But one morning three weeks after their arrival, the police stormed in and drove away with all three children. Lesley's husband had accused her of child abduction. Even though Lesley had reported his threats and violence to the police, and had followed the recommendations of a charity that specialized in domestic violence, her husband had managed to find a judge who went along with the claim that *he* was the victim. Teresa had never seen anything like it in her years at the shelter. Lesley's husband wasn't just vicious and violent but also very well connected. A member of his family had been in banking and politics during the seventies and had established the kind of influential and long-standing relationships that still managed to protect his abusive grandson four decades later. Finding a job for Lesley was the first step in helping her get her children back. I was relieved Teresa had thought of it. Even more so since Lesley spoke very good Italian and could help bridge the cultural gap that divided Benin City from rural Tuscany.

"Do you still need my help, then?" I asked Teresa, while preparing coffee in the kitchen. "You know I'm fond of the girls and am happy to come up for a couple of hours a week as a friend, if the charity can't afford to hire both of us."

"Don't worry," Teresa said. "It's perfect if you two share the job. Lesley travels each Friday morning to southern Italy to visit her kids and doesn't get back before Monday night. The operators at the women's shelter don't speak English, and I don't have the time to take this on."

Teresa told me that she'd draw up a contract for me and that we'd talk about the details as soon as she'd managed to find a quiet moment. She grabbed her bag and left, already late for an important appointment at the town hall.

I was going to be free to organize the work and my hours however I wanted, as long as I made sure everything was taken care of. Apart from the paper work, language lessons had first priority. Teresa had tried to find an Italian teacher, but the one she had contacted kept saying she didn't have time. I filled in until we could find a native speaker. I had brought along my kids' picture dictionaries and my old Italian grammar books. I had prepared paper signs to stick up in the house labeling the rooms and furniture in Italian. Fola and Izogie wouldn't be able to read them, but other inhabitants of the house could translate for them each time they walked past.

Teresa had also suggested that Hope or Joyce could help Nina with her English homework. It seemed an ideal approach; the two educated Nigerian girls helping the Italian in need of brushing up her English. In return, Nina could help them with their Italian. Sadly, they couldn't stand each other. Nina complained about their bad manners, and Hope and Joyce said Nina was lazy and never cleaned the kitchen after cooking and kept hiding behind her books instead. I tried to mediate but could see that both sides weren't entirely wrong. The first attempt at cultural integration had failed right away, and many more would follow. I started to jot down a list of things I had to discuss with Lesley: shopping, cleaning, organizing Italian lessons and other activities that would foster integration, following up on the paper work needed for the asylum requests and their health care, resolving conflicts between the two parties in the house (the most difficult and urgent one).

I joined the girls, who were lounging on the sofa. I asked about their favorites among the Swiss chocolate, while I confiscated some for Anna and her family.

"They are all too sweet," Hope said.

"Try the black Toblerone, or one of the dark Lindts. You can actually find it here too. *Cioccolato fondente* it's called in Italian, my favorite."

"That's a bit better, mum," Izogie said. "But no offense, I'd rather eat a fruit after lunch than any of your chocolate."

"Oh, good for you," I said. The Italians were big on having a piece of fruit after lunch or dinner, a custom that had never grown on me.

"So, about the party—I have an invitation for one."

"What party?" Hope asked.

"Remember I said at the hospital I'd take you dancing once you're all back at the house?"

47

"Yes, a party! But you have to get us wigs. We can't go out like this!"

"Wigs? Why would you want to wear a wig? You look great!" Hope had woven her hair into two short braids, which I had admired that morning. The girls had asked for wigs and weaves during their first week in Dogana, but I had no idea where to find them in Tuscany, and I couldn't really understand why they were asking for them in the first place. "Anyway, a friend has invited me to her party and told me to bring you along."

This wasn't entirely true. I had phoned my friend, who owned a holiday house outside of Dogana, to tell her that I was working with five young Nigerian refugees. Delfina's parties always pullulated with expat friends and open-minded locals. She worked as a lawyer and activist all around the world, and I hoped that the party could be an opportunity for the girls to meet new people and make some connections. This had already turned out to be difficult in Dogana but could be easier for the girls at my friend's, considering that they'd meet a much younger and English-speaking crowd, that was nevertheless connected to this area. It seemed a proactive approach, unconventional perhaps but not out of place, since these parties were liberal affairs for torchbearers of the hippie spirit. The more the merrier was the rule, and the more cosmopolitan, the better.

One year, Delfina had arrived at a birthday party of mine with a group of Polish musicians in tow. We had a great night, even though she hadn't bothered to tell me she would be arriving with four more people. It turned out I should have copied her approach and taken the girls along without asking, because when I mentioned that they were from Nigeria, her peace-and-love spirit suddenly showed a crack. She said she wasn't sure there would be enough food to eat for everybody. Not enough food?

This was Italy. There was always much more food than anybody could eat, and people were happy to bring something if you asked them. It was obvious that Delfina's problem wasn't the food, but I already had my foot in the door and she agreed to let us come, as long as we brought some food and made sure we all dressed up according to the *Odyssey* theme of the party. I was close to telling her that the girls didn't need costumes since they had just been on an odyssey but didn't want to risk losing out on her already hesitant invitation.

I plastered the house with my Italian stickers while the girls talked about partying, music and dancing. Izogie said she hadn't been to a party in a long time.

"How long?" I asked.

"The last time was in Nigeria, when I turned seventeen," she said. I did the math. That was three and a half years ago.

"But I can still remember how to dance." She stood up to show us.

"Mum, you look like this." Fola had joined her and made some robotic movements. "This is white people dancing!"

"And this is Naija dancing." Fola shook her booty to the applause of her friends.

Hope and Precious got up to perform alternating interpretations of Nigerian dancing and my supposed Terminator moves. They all laughed. Not me, though. My self-esteem was as shaky as most people's, but I had always felt confident about two things: I knew how to ski (not surprising for a Swiss spending a lot of time on snowy slopes), and I could dance (definitely surprising if you'd ever come across any of my three brothers on the dance floor). I was white skinned and flat bummed, but I had the moves, and these five girls half my age had better watch out.

***

Lesley got back on Tuesday. I asked about her kids. They were between seven and thirteen years old and wanted to get out of the children's home to be reunited with their mother. When they were taken away from the women's shelter, Teresa and the local police had expected them to be back soon, since this situation was unheard of and too absurd to be true. Ten months later, nothing had been resolved, and Lesley continued to travel to southern Italy once a week to visit her children.

"I hope the new job and work contract will speed things up at last," I said.

"My lawyer says a good contract definitely helps. And working here keeps me sane. These girls are a handful, but it takes my mind away from all the difficulties I'm dealing with. I have been waiting and praying for nearly a year. At least here I can do something."

***

Sergio, the kids and I picked the girls up on Saturday night. Hope and Izogie were in the kitchen, and the chicken was still simmering on the stove. Lesley had schlepped a huge bag of rice from her trip to Rome, and I had brought lots of pepper, since there was never enough of it in the house. I hadn't figured out yet whether Nigerians used black pepper, chili pepper or some other African, and to me unknown, pepper in their cooking. But the *peperoncini*, the little red chili peppers I brought up from our garden, were always welcome and used up very quickly. I had also gone through my wardrobe and collected two bags of clothes, shoes and scarves for them. We wouldn't have the most imaginative costumes at the party, but I wanted them to be able to have fun and dress up.

"No lipstick, mum?" Izogie was trying on some of my earrings. She wore a gold sequin dress that had been stored in a garment bag in our attic for years, since I could never find the right occasion to wear it.

Joyce asked me to wrap a headscarf for her. I was surprised. Joyce had hardly talked to me so far. I imagined her to be either very shy or very traumatized. Or maybe she just didn't like me. Joyce had a pretty, round face, and her short, plump body still showed a bit of baby fat, the exact opposite of skinny and long-boned Precious, with whom she hung out the most. I had asked the girls on the first day to write down their names for me, and Joyce had passed on the paper without writing anything. I had deduced that she couldn't write, but it turned out later that she and Hope had received the most schooling. I was happy that I was able to do something for her, even though I was sure she had more experience with wrapping up a headscarf than me.

The giant turban I had tied around my head in my reconstruction of Trojan fashion in the times of Cassandra was already coming loose, as my children kept pointing out to me. They were the only ones who had refused to dress up. Costumes were, according to them, something for carnival, not an end-of-summer party. I was with them on this one, unlike Sergio, who looked surprisingly attractive as a male Siren. The girls complimented his pink tulle hair and glittery beard while the nine of us squeezed into our seven-seater station wagon. Sergio turned on the radio and steered our intercontinental motley crew and two huge pots of jollof rice past cypress trees into the midst of a Tuscan odyssey—improvised turbans and makeshift wigs shaking from all the laughter.

5

"I can't find Fola."

Lesley's phone call had woken me up in the middle of the night. She had just gotten back to the house in Dogana after visiting her kids at the children's home in southern Italy.

"Wait," I switched on the light and sat up in bed, "what did you say?"

"We can't find her. She isn't here. The girls came down when I got in an hour ago. We had a chat in the kitchen, but Fola didn't join us. After awhile, I asked why and the girls said she must be in bed. I didn't make anything of it and put on my pajamas. Then I suddenly thought, *This is strange, I better check.* I went upstairs and couldn't find her in her bed or anywhere else."

Shit, was all I could think of. *Shit, shit, shit.*

I got up to put the kettle on. I had known this could happen, but I hadn't expected it to happen so quickly.

"What about her things?"

"Her bag and clothes are still in the room."

After arriving in Sicily, the girls had been given printed sports club bags that matched their referee tracksuits. Each bag had contained no more than a couple of T-shirts, a pair of flip-flops, a towel and a change of underwear. But once the girls were in Tuscany, the bags had started to fill up with pieces from the Red Cross heap and hand-me-downs from Lesley and me that they seemed to like.

I checked my watch. "Maybe she's still out on town?" It was a faint hope. Partying into the early hours was not an option in a small hilltop town with a population with a median age of sixty-five.

"The keys are all in the house," Lesley said.

"But if she left, why did she go without her bag?"

"I guess she didn't want anybody to notice that she was planning to leave."

Lesley was right. Fola couldn't have packed her bag without being asked some questions by me or somebody else in the house.

"But what about the girls?" I asked. "They said she was asleep. Were they covering for her?"

"I don't think so. You know how they swap beds and rooms all the time? Hope and Joyce said that they thought Fola was sleeping in the other room for the night."

Where was she going? She had left without her bag. She didn't have a phone. And no documents. Lesley and I had tried to hammer it in stone: don't trust anybody and don't even think of leaving the refugee home before you have your documents. The girls kept answering that they didn't have the least intention of leaving.

"Do you think she'll come back?" I asked.

"I don't know. She's a funny girl."

"She may want to, once she realizes what kind of mess she's getting herself into."

"Yes, she may want to," Lesley said. "But it's probably going to be too late by then."

I made myself a cup of tea and decided to call Teresa in the morning. She would have to inform the prefecture, but there was no point in getting her out of bed in the middle of the night. Unless Fola reappeared during the next five days, the prefecture would not let her back into the project. And if she made it back in time, she'd get a warning. She had signed the project contract and been informed that refugees weren't allowed to stay away overnight without giving prior notice to the staff.

I swiped through the pictures on my smartphone. There were a few hilarious shots of Fola in a sarong and one of my bikini tops at the beach. None of the girls had ever been to the sea before coming to Italy. They had been on it during their nightmare crossing, but they had never spent a day at the beach, enjoying the sun. We had organized a little excursion the day after they had received their first pocket money. Refugees got 2.50 euros per day from the government, and after rounding up a bit, by the end of August the girls got paid 80 euros each. They bought moisturizer, nail polish and a couple of other small things and put the rest aside for a phone. I had given them my old Nokia, but what they needed more than anything was a smartphone.

Hope had managed to check Facebook on the Nokia phone's browser (I never quite understood how), but WhatsApp, Skype and other big money savers for international communications were only available on recent models. We spent a morning at a shopping center going through the different options. Izogie bought a simple phone to try with her Libyan SIM card, which she had hidden in her bra during the passage on the boat. The others decided to wait, since they weren't able to buy an Italian SIM card until they received their first document in the form of a temporary permit of stay. We discussed cheap phone plans and drove to the beach, where the girls changed into random pieces of my bikinis mixed in with their underwear or a sarong. They paraded up and down the shore, snapping countless pictures with my phone while striking suggestive Nollywood movie star poses. A small blonde German girl with a plastic shovel could be seen in a couple of pictures. She looked in awe at Precious, Hope, Izogie, Joyce and Fola, who were artfully positioned around her. None of my Nigerian beach companions could swim, but Fola waded bravely through the water and asked to take lessons with me until I promised that I would teach her one day. Why had she left?

Just like me, the last time the girls had seen Fola was during our Italian class on the day she disappeared. There had been a call for her on the house phone towards the end of the lesson. A male voice with a Nigerian accent. Fola took the phone up to her room and didn't come back down before I left. We had hardly done any Italian, since I had spent most of the class questioning and discussing the girls' behavior at my friend's party. Even though Fola had been the most out of control, I was especially annoyed at the other girls, whom I had asked to keep an eye on their friend. Fola throwing up all over the nicely trimmed lawn had been bad enough. I didn't want her to stagger off and fall in the pool. But Joyce, Hope and Precious just kept chatting at a nearby table without ever checking on her. I intercepted Izogie on the dance floor with the same request. She didn't want to hear it and suggested that we should take Fola back to the house—obviously mistaking Sergio and me for an on-demand taxi service. I made it clear during our lesson that I hadn't been hired to chaperone drunk refugees. Especially if they couldn't even be bothered to take care of each other.

"We are not friends, mum," Joyce had said. "We happened to be on the same boat and have ended up here together. We are not family or friends and are not responsible for anybody's behavior."

Fola had already left the room, but Izogie, Precious and Hope nodded in agreement. Joyce was less loud and outspoken than the others. She was the youngest in the group and had sneaked off from the party with a bottle of Prosecco under her scarf. Nevertheless, she seemed the most calm and responsible of the five.

I went back to bed and tried to stop thinking about Fola. After all, there wasn't anything to be done. One didn't call the carabinieri at two in the morning for a refugee gone amiss. What were they supposed to do? A young Nigerian woman on the loose, one more illegal immigrant roaming Italy without a document—who cared? Missing persons statements were for people who had had a life. Who had been part of something that they could get back to, who were in fact *missed* by somebody.

II

Autumn

6

Izogie told me to take a right turn and follow the road for a bit. We were on our way to the police station to pick up the girls' first permit of stay, but after fifteen years of living in Tuscany, I still managed to get lost. I knew every backroad in the historic town center but always lost my bearings in the less appealing parts of the city built in the seventies and eighties.

"There it is, mum."

The colossal building hosting the immigration office appeared at the end of the road. Izogie's directions had been right. She had been at the office twice since her arrival in Italy. The first time to be fingerprinted after arriving in Tuscany from Sicily. The second time with me on the day we had lodged the girls' official asylum request.

"Thank you, Izogie."

"No problem, mum. Just ask."

It seemed that the difficulty of having to get through life without books and education was in Izogie's case partly redeemed by an excellent sense of orientation. Should I ever be forced to flee Europe and find my way to safety by crossing countries where I couldn't read the street signs, I wanted to do it in the company of Izogie.

I parked the car in front of the steps leading up to the police headquarters. The immigration office was located in a modern and particularly uninviting building—the architect had managed to reflect in his design the uneasiness most people suffered when entering it. Walking up the steps behind the girls, I told Precious to pull down her T-shirt. She was wearing a pair of opaque tights but no skirt. We had to line up, which gave me time to explain the difference between leggings and tights, and why skintight leggings were acceptable when worn on their own and tights—opaque or not—weren't.

"Mum, we got it!" Hope said, and Precious and Joyce walked to the other side of the room to sit down on the plastic chairs in the waiting area.

I was never sure whether they cut me off because they felt patronized by my little speeches about different cultural rules or because cutting me off was their way of patronizing me. Perhaps they were just normal youngsters easily bored by the never-ending sermons of a Swiss woman twice their age.

The lineup moved, and Joyce, Hope, Izogie, Fola and Precious were handed their first *permessi di soggiorno*, permits of stay valid for three months. I asked the officer behind the window when we would have to come back to renew it.

"A month before it expires."

"A month before it expires?" I checked the dates on Hope and Izogie's permits. They were valid from the day we made the request in August, even though the documents had been ready to be picked up only a month and a half later. "But that would mean we'd have to come back next week?"

"Yes," he said, without lifting his head from the papers in front of him. "And remember to bring new photos and tax stamps for all of them."

I couldn't believe we had to plan another drive to the city for another round of photos and another *marca da bollo* (a tax stamp costing sixteen euros each) for a permit that would—again—be valid for only three months and hence be nearly expired when we picked it up.

I was swearing under my breath when we left the office, but the girls didn't mind. They were holding the first document of identification they had ever possessed. They chatted and laughed about each other's photos while getting into the car.

"I wish Fola had at least waited for her permit of stay," I said, before I turned on the engine.

"Mum," Izogie said, "Fola isn't right in the head."

"Forget that girl," Hope added from the back. "She's no good."

The day after Fola's disappearance, I had asked the girls whether they knew what might have happened, why she might have run away. They all insisted that they didn't know anything about it. They didn't want to talk about it, and when I asked whether they were worried about her, they said no. Fola was—according to them—a lazy fool, who had never even helped with the cleaning. I asked Lesley about it, and she agreed. Fola hadn't been easy to deal with in the house and always had a lame excuse ready when asked to help or contribute anything. But did that mean she wasn't to be supported and looked out for? The topic reminded me of a conversation I had had with a friend who had been at the *Odyssey* party. She had been appalled that the Nigerian girls hadn't behaved better. Since they're status was precarious as asylum seekers, the gathering could have been their chance to leave a good impression and perhaps secure a job for the future. I agreed with her, since one reason why I had taken them to the party was that I had hoped for the same thing, but I also realized then how absurd our expectations were. The Italians and expats of their age were allowed to party and go crazy as much as they wanted, but the refugees attending the celebration had to behave impeccably and prove to everybody that they were nice and responsible. Refugees had a very narrow path of appropriate behavior they were allowed to walk on, even though they, much more than me or any of my friends, had reason to properly celebrate after all the perils they had managed to survive.

"Girls, I know I said in the past that if you wanted to leave, at least wait 'til you have your documents. That doesn't mean that you should run off now."

"Mum," Joyce said, "just because we're all Nigerians, doesn't mean we'll all behave like Fola."

"I know, but—"

"Mum!" they all yelled.

"Okay, okay."

But was it? We had had several conversations about human trafficking and the exploitation of Nigerian women in Italy and Europe. Lesley had called a friend of hers who had been a victim of a prostitution ring. She had asked each of the girls to talk to her on the phone. She wanted them to know exactly what it was like out there on the road. The point we wanted to make was that we didn't have a moral problem with the issue. If they wanted to work as prostitutes, we wouldn't object. But we wanted them to be aware of what the reality would look like. The reports I had read said that the young women from Edo State often knew from the start that they would have to work as prostitutes in Europe to pay off their debt. But I didn't imagine that the traffickers took the time to explain under what miserable conditions they'd be working. That working for a madam didn't mean making a lot of money but spending interminable hours waiting for clients on the side of an Italian road. In every season and at every time of day. Without documents and without a phone. And most importantly, with nobody looking for them, should anything happen. They could easily be replaced with a new girl, and no pimp or madam would tell the police that one of their illegal workers had gone missing. Lesley had been contacted several times by Nigerian families looking for their daughters. The story was always the same. They had not heard from the girl in a long time, or even since she left Nigeria in the first place. Lesley had reported the cases to the Nigerian embassy in Rome, where she was told that so many girls and young women disappeared every year that there was no point in even trying to start looking for them. At the refugee home, the reactions to our talks were always the same. The girls didn't want to hear about it. We "accused" them of something they had nothing to do with. They were in Europe because of Boko Haram. My insinuations offended them. And they were bored to death by our lectures about the dangers of life as sex workers. Nevertheless, Fola had disappeared exactly in the way I had feared, and I thought we had to keep making the point.

I had been looking for support from more experienced people in the field and had contacted Be Free, an organization in Rome battling human trafficking and the exploitation of women. Previously, a lawyer working for Be Free had won a case against a Nigerian prostitution ring. It had been an important step forward, since the assets paid for with money earned through exploitation went to the women who had been taken advantage of. In the past, cars, apartments and other possessions owned by pimps and traffickers were given to the state. Getting back what had been taken or withheld from them provided a strong incentive for women who had been threatened and abused to muster the courage to sue their madam.

However, what I had been looking for didn't exist. After at least two decades of Nigerian trafficking in Europe, a lot of reports about the phenomenon and the ratification of the Palermo Trafficking Protocol by the United Nations, I had hoped to find a prevention scheme. But there was no structured approach addressing the very particular issues most of the young Nigerian women arriving at the reception centers were known to face once they were in Europe. Even though their situation was totally different from that of refugees arriving from Syria or Eritrea, they were undergoing exactly the same procedure. This seemed like a waste of time and resources. There were several organizations that were active in supporting girls who wanted to get off the road, but I could not find any NGO that provided guidelines for how to support refugees who didn't want to get on it in the first place. Nigerian trafficking was not a new phenomenon. Young Nigerian women had been sex workers on Italy's roads and in Europe's red light districts for more than twenty years. This was widely known. Research papers had been published that highlighted the criminal mechanisms that had taken over what might have started once as an individually organized activity. But the knowledge gained still hadn't changed the way the government handled the situation, even though continually growing numbers of young Nigerian women were arriving on Italy's shores.

I drove the girls to a shopping center, where thanks to their new permits of stay, they could at last buy SIM cards. The phone line at the refugee home had been disconnected. The girls had made too many phone calls on it, even though Lesley and I had kept telling them that the phone was to be used only for receiving calls. Anna and her children had been using the phone for national calls all along, but the girls calling family in Nigeria and friends stuck in Libya had quickly run up a hefty bill.

I dropped them at the shopping center and drove on to a

meeting with the operators of several refugee homes in southern Tuscany. A doctor from the national health services was holding a meeting about Ebola. Hospital staff was undergoing training for swift and efficient response in the event of the arrival of a patient with Ebola. Even though the doctor was proud of the service, he asked everyone to treat the news confidentially, so as to avoid feeding the media hype about the deathly epidemic. He was sure that Ebola was not going to arrive with people who reached Europe after a long trip by foot, bus and boat, as the disease killed quickly. He was to be proved right. More than 130,000 refugees arrived on Italy's shores in 2014. But the one person treated for Ebola in Italy was not a refugee but an Italian doctor, who after being infected in Sierra Leone, was urgently taken home by plane.

7

September had been a good month. At least once I had accepted that Fola wouldn't be coming back. The tension between the Italian and Nigerian inhabitants of the refugee home was still a daily issue, but having Lesley in the house made things easier. She got along well with Anna and her children, and agreed with them: the young Nigerians in the house needed to step up and take responsibility for their part of the chores. Lesley showed them how to use the washing machine and insisted the girls stop washing everything in the clogged bathroom basins. And she thoroughly cleaned the stainless-steel industrial kitchen and the rest of the house with them before her weekly visit with her children. The kitchen was always a mess when she got back, but she was on their case and expected more from the girls than I did. She wanted the Nigerians in the house to be on their best behavior. These weren't her people, though. As an Igbo from Delta State, Lesley didn't share a common culture, language or ancestry with the girls from Benin City. They were all Edo, with the exception of Fola, whose mother had been Yoruba, and Hope, who belonged to one of the ethnic groups from Rivers State. The girls represented Lesley's nation but not her people. The British colonialists had squeezed the territories they had conquered along the Niger River into one madly heterogeneous country, a nation that would never have been born had the Igbo, Yoruba, Hausa or any other of the more than three hundred ethnic groups in the assembled area been asked.

Lesley was in charge of running the house, and I took care of the bureaucracy (permits of stay, national health insurance cards) and the organization of activities. I had at last managed to find an Italian teacher. Martina, a young Italian woman who had studied and worked in Holland for several years, volunteered to take on the language classes. I had been surprised that Teresa couldn't offer any payment for this. The charity received thirty-five euros per refugee per day, but paying a language teacher was too costly, even though Teresa had reassured Lesley and me that the charity could absolutely afford hiring both of us. Learning Italian seemed one of the most important things for the Nigerian girls, and I made a mental note to find out more about this from Teresa, but I never did. The charity was already on a financial roller coaster that was swerving into full-blown disaster.

Apart from language classes, I tried to organize other activities that could prove helpful for the girls' future. I wrote emails to friends asking for computers, English books, dictionaries, DVDs (for teaching and leisure), old phones/smartphones and easy-to-read Italian children's books. I had already emailed a few friends and acquaintances about English books and warm clothes for the winter, but there hadn't been a bounty so far. Most people seemed too busy with their lives to sort through old clothes and bring over books, or they had just sorted through their clothes and already dropped them off at one of the Red Cross bins. Clothes that would be flown to Africa, before we could get our hands on them.

However, a friend moving back to England had donated a sewing machine and two boxes of fabrics. There were a couple of elderly ladies in the village who had worked as seamstresses, and I hoped to convince them to teach the girls how to use the sewing machine during the winter. And Nadia, a South African friend living in Tuscany, volunteered, for everybody's well-being, to teach a weekly yoga lesson. The house had a nice gym space from its time as a rehabilitation center, and a physiotherapist still taught gymnastics there to the village seniors.

Izogie needed special support for literacy. The Italian lessons were hardest for her, since she couldn't read and write. She was able to spell her name, had a basic knowledge of the alphabet and was very keen to learn. She had been made fun of for not knowing how to read and write her whole life. I had also put her name down for a project I wanted to get back to in spring—the school garden at the women's shelter in the countryside. We had spent a few afternoons at an alpaca farm nearby, an unusual but interesting adventure in Tuscany. The only girl interested had been Izogie. The others hadn't come to Europe to break their backs working the fields. Izogie was the only one who had grown up in the countryside before moving to Benin City. Her parents used to farm a plot of land, but both had died early. An uncle had taken on the land but not his brother's daughter.

Izogie was the most physical and practical of the girls in the house. Everybody else showed so little stamina during the yoga lessons that I doubted they could keep up a day's worth of hard physical work in a Tuscan vineyard or olive grove. I knew what they would be in for. I had had a go at farm work during my first year in Tuscany and had failed miserably.

The various projects we were doing were often short-lived, since my days in Dogana were spent mostly crossing bureaucratic hurdles and sorting out the conflicts arising between the people living in the house. Unlike many other refugee homes, the small size of ours meant that our guests could cook for themselves. A fact they cherished a lot. Once a week, the groceries arrived and we had to make sure everything was split evenly between the Italians and Nigerians. Both parties had taken to storing food in their bedrooms, as they didn't trust the other party when they left a packet of rice or a can of tomatoes in the kitchen. There was never enough food by the end of the week, and this was obviously a problem. Teresa told me they had to learn to make do with the things that were available. I insisted what was available wasn't enough. I knew how the trunk of our car looked when it was filled with the weekly shopping for our family. The food the charity passed on to me once a week to take up to the refugee home took up the same space in my car as our food shopping for a family of four (two of whom were kids). The girls kept protesting, and rightly so. They had had a lot of problems where they came from, but food had never been one of them. They asked whether they could have the money to do the shopping on their own. I explained that it didn't make sense, since the small village shops in Dogana were much more expensive than the wholesale the charity went to in the city. But I knew something had to change.

"Mum, you have to tell Teresa," Izogie said. "We never see her."

"She's busy. That's why she hired me to work things out with you. But I'm not in charge of the money. I have to speak with her first."

"We know you're not in charge of the money. That's why she has to come here and talk to us."

"Teresa is under a lot of pressure. But I'll make sure I sort this out with her."

"Tell her that we want to do the shopping ourselves. We are old enough to work it out!"

"I don't think it will work for all of the shopping, since that would become too expensive. But if there are some things each week that you can buy at the *alimentari*, the grocer's in town—great!"

The more things they took charge of themselves, the better. And doing a bit of the shopping at the village shops would have been a good thing for the locals too, since the shopowners who struggled to make a living would welcome any new customer. And the girls would get more chances to meet people from the village.

I promised to talk to Teresa and heard from her on the same day. She asked me to pass by her office in the town hall for a meeting. I knew we had a problem if she had called me. It had become hard to get ahold of Teresa. She was buried in work, and I normally had to call and text her several times before she'd answer the phone. I drove to the town hall right away.

"One of the members of the council has reported complaints from the villagers about the girls," Teresa said.

"What did they complain about?"

"The girls were seen buying alcohol at the local shop."

"That's not ideal, but everybody their age drinks alcohol here."

"Right, but it seems they are also trying to sell sex."

"Who says that?"

"The village rumor mill."

"Do you know who started that rumor?"

"No. It's impossible to know whether it's true or that's what the village thinks is true because the girls are black, young and—"

"And walking around in tights without skirts, I know."

I went straight back to the house. I opened the door and heard loud laughter when I walked up the stairs. The girls were having an Italian class with Martina. I waited for the class to finish and talked to Anna in the meantime.

"Teresa told me that there are rumors in the village that the girls prostitute themselves. Have you heard anything?"

"No, I haven't."

"Have you seen them drinking?"

"Drinking?"

"Alcohol, here in the house?"

"I'm not sure. Maybe last week. They were very loud one night. But you know how they are. They are always loud."

Anna and her family had complained about their shouting before. They were right; Nigerians were loud. But it also made me laugh, because "They are too loud" was exactly what the Swiss used to say in the sixties and seventies when an Italian family moved into a neighborhood.

I went upstairs and checked the girls' bedrooms. A half-empty bottle of sambuca was standing on the table in the middle of bottles of shampoo and Nivea containers in Izogie and Precious's bedroom.

I heard Martina say good-bye and went downstairs with the bottle.

"Mum?" Joyce said.

"We have to talk." I pulled up a chair and joined the girls at the table where they had had the Italian lesson.

"Where did you get the sambuca?" I asked, holding up the bottle.

"At the shop in town," Hope said.

"Please, don't buy more of it."

"You said this morning, it's good if we use the local stores!" Precious said.

"You said it's good if we meet some locals!" Joyce added.

"I didn't quite recommend buying high-percentage alcohol so as to meet the locals. If you want to have a glass, go to the bar

71

like the Italians do."

"Mum, the bar is too expensive," Izogie said. "It's cheaper if we buy a bottle at the shop and drink it at home."

"I know, but it doesn't work like that here. People will think you're drunkards if you buy a bottle of grappa or sambuca at the shop."

Liquor stores weren't part of traditional Tuscan village life. Alcohol could be purchased in the small village stores, but young women, Italian or not, were talked about if they bought a bottle of high-percentage alcohol. Wine was consumed at home with a meal; otherwise, people mostly went to the local bar to have a drink. Or several. Even the smallest village had a bar where people met for a stand-up coffee in the morning, an aperitif before a meal and a game of cards, or yet another glass after dinner. Italian bars used to be men-only affairs, and in the countryside, this had started to change only recently.

"Do you remember the contract you signed when you moved in here?" I said. "It says you're not allowed to smoke or drink in the house."

"We don't smoke," Joyce said.

"I know, but you can't drink in here either."

"Mum, we just had a bit of fun on Saturday night!"

"I understand. But from now on, please respect the contract and don't bring alcohol into the house." I wondered what my twenty-year-old self would have said to that. I shared a flat with a couple of drama school students in the center of Zurich when I was their age. Nobody seemed to mind that we partied a lot. That's what aspiring artists do. But expectations were different for refugees. Which reminded me of something else.

"And also, remember that you can't bring guests into the house. You'll have to tell us first if you have family or close friends who'd like to visit."

"Okay, mum," Hope said, while looking through the apps on her new smartphone.

"Have you invited anybody into the house without telling us?"

"No, mum, why?"

"Some people in the village say you are selling sex." A tidal wave of shouting hit me. I waited for it to die down and realized that these were issues better tackled in one-on-one conversations.

"Mum, people say things like this just because we're black. Every black woman is a prostitute to them."

"They don't even greet us."

"They think we want to sell sex, even if we just say hello to be polite."

"I know," I said. "It sucks."

No doubt, some villagers were having wet dreams since the girls had arrived. Nevertheless, I had no clue what to believe. Two of the first words Joyce had asked me to translate during our Italian classes in August had been "love" and "money." It may have been a coincidence. These were two words most young people living abroad would want to know. But still.

Anna told me a few days later that she had gotten home early one morning after working a night shift at the hospital. She arrived in Dogana at 6 AM and saw Hope slipping into the house just before her. Hope told me afterward that she had gone for a walk. She had not been feeling well and couldn't sleep at night.

***

Hope hadn't been sleeping well since she first arrived. By the end of September, she wasn't just lying awake at night but also complaining about feeling nauseous, tired and bloated.

"Have you had your period this month?"

"No, mum."

"Last month?"

"No, mum. I haven't had my period since we arrived in Italy."

"Darn, you should have told me."

"I was often missing it in Libya too."

"What happened in Libya?"

"You know the school I went to? The fashion school I showed you on Google Maps in the hospital?"

"Yes, I remember."

"My mother didn't have the money to pay for me to finish the school. I had to stop. But after a few months, my aunt called from Libya. She said I could finish studying in Tripoli. She would pay for the school."

"That's why you went to Tripoli?"

"Yes, I had only a year left to get my diploma. She sent the money for the trip. When I arrived, my aunt told me we had to meet somebody before she could take me to the school. She took me to the house I told you about. The house where they locked me up until I got to Italy."

"What happened in the house?"

"Mum!"

"Why were you locked up?"

"What do you think happens if they lock up twenty girls in a small apartment in Libya? They made us work. Pay for the trip they said. Men were coming all the time."

"You couldn't get out?"

"They beat you up for everything. Imagine trying to run away."

"What happened to your aunt?"

"She left."

"She left?"

"She took the money and ran."

"What money?"

"Mum!"

"What? I don't get it. You mean she sold you?"

"There was no fashion school in Libya."

"But you said she was your aunt."

"I think she was in trouble. I guess she needed the money."

***

Hope took a pregnancy test. She wasn't pregnant. The doctor prescribed sleeping pills for her instead.

8

The girls looked great when I picked them up. They were all dressed up and wearing the weaves, braids and wigs Lesley had bought for them in Rome. Precious had worked as a hairdresser in Nigeria and had been busy for days with everybody's new hairstyles. A whole universe of questions opened up in front of me when I inspected Hope's glossy weave of long, straight black hair. I knew that Tina Turner always wore a wig, but I had always interpreted it as an artistic choice. But what about Michelle Obama, or Naomi Campbell? I had only recently learned from Lesley, who always wore a weave, that a lot of black women went to great lengths to hide or straighten their hair. I hadn't been aware that centuries of oppression and slavery were still finding a contemporary expression in the rejection of black women's natural hair. I started to tell the girls that I thought it was a shame that they covered their beautiful hair. And that they could do better things with their pocket money than investing it in fake hair extensions and a collection of wigs. But considering Naomi Campbell probably wouldn't have become a supermodel if she hadn't hidden her natural hair, and Barack Obama might not have become president if Michelle didn't straighten hers, it was naïve of me to think that the girls would choose to forgo wigs and weaves as an act of emancipation or protest (and that I was a white woman trying to encourage them wasn't without irony).

"Joyce, where's your jacket?"

"I don't need one, mum. I'm not cold." She was wearing only the printed T-shirt she had bought the last time we were in the city.

"You're not cold now, but you will be tonight, as soon as the sun goes down."

"I'll be fine, mum."

Yeah, I thought. With the temperatures dropping, I had gotten used to keeping a few extra jackets and scarves in the car. My frequent suggestions to dress in layers wasn't met with much interest.

In the car, Precious worked a bit of stray hair back into Joyce's weave. I signaled to Izogie to keep her voice down. She and Hope were both talking loudly into their new phones. I started the engine and caught a glimpse of my short, mousy hair in the rearview mirror. It wasn't a nice sight in the midst of all the glamorous hairdos.

During the drive to my village, I pointed out the highlights of Tuscany's festival tradition: wine, chestnut and olive oil harvest festivals took place from September to early December. Each Tuscan village in the area had its own weekend of harvest bounty that managed to turn remote ghost towns into upbeat localities with live music and bars staying open until late into the night.

"Eh, mum," Hope had finished her phone call. "What were you saying?"

"I said you'll have a lot of fun tonight. Our village is well known for its crazy harvest festival."

We started the evening in good Italian tradition with an aperitif at the local bar. Joyce ordered a Coke, and Hope, Izogie and Precious chose an ice cream from the freezer.

"Sure you don't want a glass of Prosecco?' Everybody else in the bar was already on their third or fourth round of Campari.

"Mum, you told us not to drink," Precious said, unwrapping her Cornetto.

"That's not what I meant. I said you can't drink at the refugee home."

Izogie pulled a crumpled tissue from her bag. She unfolded it carefully and pushed the fine white powder hidden in it over to my side of the table. "Do you want some, mum?"

I nearly fell off my barstool.

Sex, drugs and rock 'n' roll. I should have known. Our yoga teacher had told me about drug trafficking being in Nigerian hands in South Africa, and I had just come across a newspaper article that mentioned the territorial fights in Naples between the Camorra crime syndicate and the Nigerian Mafia.

"Put it away!" The last thing I needed was the whole village, and the two carabinieri, the national police officers who were having an espresso at the counter, looking on while four black refugees and I started the local harvest festival by snorting cocaine. The girls regarded me with surprise. It obviously hadn't occurred to them that this wasn't appropriate behavior in a Tuscan village bar. "Put it away, right now!"

Izogie pulled the tissue slowly back across the table, put two fingers into the powder and patted her forehead and cheekbones before checking her reflection in the mirror behind the counter.

"That's better," said Hope.

I watched Izogie's skillful use of her makeshift compact and felt like a fool—and immensely relieved that I had not accepted her invitation to try some of the powder in the tissue: a middle-aged Swiss woman getting high sniffing lines of talcum powder at the local bar would have made the annals of our town. Sergio still regaled everyone with the story of a friend who had managed to sell sheep dung for hashish late one night thirty years ago. I would have joined the long line of countryside dwellers who, removed from the main trafficking hubs of the cities, managed to get high on the most unlikely substances.

We left the bar to visit Sergio, who was cooking with his best friend in a cantina, one of the old cellars that were cleaned out and opened up for the festival each autumn. I took the girls for a tour of several cellars, before we walked up to a little square to meet their Italian teacher. A DJ was in the square, and Martina was dancing with her fiancé and friends who had flown in from Holland for the weekend of the festival. We joined them on the medieval dance floor, but Joyce was cold and wanted to go back home. I went to the car to get her a jacket. When I came back, the Dutch had taken over the DJ table, and Hope and Joyce took turns singing karaoke with them. I asked Izogie and Precious why they didn't join in, realizing too late that Izogie couldn't read the lyrics. Precious could but wasn't interested. She wanted to go home.

"Why?"

"I'm tired."

"You must be kidding. You're always up late in the house. Has anything happened?"

"No, I just want to go home."

"Come on, everybody is having fun with the karaoke. I'll take you home in a bit, but you'll have to sing a song first."

I was still having a hard time with Precious. She was aloof and downright impolite, but each time I overheard her singing in the house I stopped to listen. Her voice—warm and smoky—was the opposite of the ill-mannered young woman who hardly greeted me when I saw her at the house. Precious sang melancholic tunes in a language I couldn't understand when she was cooking or cleaning (which didn't happen often, unless we pestered her). I had asked a friend, a singer and piano teacher, whether she could find the time to meet Precious in autumn. Maybe music was the way to get through to her.

The girls gave an encore on the square before they greeted Martina and her friends. They had had a blast and were shrieking and laughing during the drive back to Dogana. I reminded them to dress in comfortable clothes the next day since they had agreed to help me at the festival restaurant on Saturday night.

"What do you mean by comfortable, mum?" Joyce asked.

"Just don't wear your nicest things. You might stain them in the kitchen or while waiting tables."

**

"Where are you?"

"At the bar."

"I asked you to be at the festival restaurant by eight o'clock."

"Okay, mum, we'll leave now."

They didn't. The restaurant was filling up quickly, and we were buried under an onslaught of orders. I called again.

"Izogie, where are you? We need help here."

"We'll be there in a minute."

There weren't enough people in the kitchen. I had counted on Precious, Izogie, Hope and Joyce to help. They arrived towards nine o'clock.

"Mum, what can we do?" Izogie asked.

"Take an apron each. Izogie and Joyce, you help cutting the bread for the bruschetta. Hope and Precious, you can start cleaning the tables with me. We need space for the next round of people to sit down for dinner."

I showed Izogie and Joyce how to cut the bread. The big Tuscan loaves had just arrived from the bakery and were still hot and difficult to handle, but Izogie made an effort and worked it out. Unlike Hope and Precious, who were sitting at one of the tables they were supposed to clean. I was speechless.

"Mum, we already cleaned a table over there."

They had, but in the meantime, four more tables had been freed up, which we needed for the customers waiting in the lineup.

"Come on, girls, give me a hand with this!" I asked Hope to hold open a big black garbage bag. She watched me scrape leftovers from the plates into the trash and looked disgusted.

"Are you doing this for free?"

"Yes. Nobody here is paid. I thought I had explained that. We're all doing voluntary work for the village."

"All these people running around like that for free?" Precious had joined us at the trash can and studied the Italians hurrying by. "I don't believe you."

"We are here to support the village and the community. And it would be a good moment for you to show that you appreciate being here."

I walked back indoors and emptied my tray. Izogie had cut her finger, which had slipped from the thick crust of Tuscan bread. None of the girls was used to eating bread, nor had they ever cut any.

"Is it bad?"

"No, don't worry mum."

I got a tissue and told Izogie to sit down with Hope and Precious, who had stopped cleaning the moment I walked away. Joyce joined us and asked whether I could take them home. They had been helping at the restaurant for less than an hour and were exhausted. So was I. Integration via partying—I had to let it go. Whether celebrating friends' birthdays or helping out during village festivals—it wasn't working. I told the girls that they'd have to wait for the end of my shift and promised myself to stop being their driver. Traumatized or not, they had to start pulling their weight.

9

And then there were none.

The children's verse was stuck in my head all through the yoga lesson at the refugee home. Its rhymes accompanied me through the positions of the sun salutation like the refrain of an irritating pop song. Then there were five, upward hand pose, then there were four, forward bend, then there were three, upward-facing dog. It was sobering to see what connections my brain made each time one of our Nigerian girls disappeared. Regardless of my political and social views, my brain had been hardwired during a childhood in the seventies, a time when racist nursery rhymes were still a staple of the artfully illustrated books aimed at educating and entertaining Europe's toddlers. I was reminded of this when looking through my childhood library with my own children. Too attached to the extravagant graphics of the seventies to throw the offenders out, I hid the books before my kids could put their hands on them. I wanted their brains to be free of associations like these. But it was too late for mine.

Precious had gone missing on the last Thursday in October. The girls had been in the city in the morning and were supposed to get back in the early afternoon. They had missed the bus and arrived late for yoga. And there were only three of them. Precious had not gotten on the bus. She had told Hope, Izogie and Joyce that she had already informed me that she'd come back later. We had had several discussions during October because the girls kept arriving late or not at all to Italian and yoga lessons. I had warned them that we'd hold off the pocket money on the days they skipped lessons without giving advance notice and a good reason why they were not able to make it. But contrary to what she had told the girls at the bus stop in town, Precious had not called me. It was obvious: she wouldn't be coming back.

I worried less about Precious's disappearance than I had about Fola's, possibly because I had never gotten along with her in the first place. Or perhaps I was just getting used to losing girls along the way. I kept asking Joyce about Precious.

"Did you know she was planning to leave? Have you tried to call her?"

"No."

"She doesn't answer the phone when I call her, but she might answer a call from you. The two of you seemed to get along well."

"She wasn't my friend, mum." Joyce looked up from the stack of Nollywood movies Lesley had bought for her mum and the girls. "She didn't tell me anything."

"And she has run off before repaying her debts!" Izogie added. They both had lent Precious some of their monthly pocket money to buy a smartphone the three of them were supposed to share. Precious had left all her belongings at the house. Apart from the phone.

Lesley and I couldn't figure out whether the girls didn't want to talk about Precious and Fola because they had known they would run off sooner or later, or because they wanted to make sure they were not associated with any "wrongdoing." My interpretation of the situation was steeped in the ideals and emotional baggage of a forty-two-year-old middle-class woman with two kids. One of them a daughter for whom all I wanted was the exact opposite of what these girls were probably facing. It was a mess. Things had seemed much more straightforward when I had first met them. In July, they had seemed like a group of young women who were escaping a crazy fundamentalist crowd in West Africa. A few months later, I tried to keep five, four and now three young Nigerian women from giving blow jobs to Tuscan seniors at roadside stops. I no longer worried about Boko Haram—nasty bearded men who had lost their bearings in absurd interpretations of an ancient book seemed much less of a threat in the Tuscan outback than truck drivers and Italian family men looking for a quickie during their lunch break.

At least our yoga teacher would have an easier time now with one less pupil. Precious had sulked her way through every single one of Nadia's lessons. She could not see the point in yoga. It seemed to me that Precious could not see the point in anything that wasn't a new phone, a funky weave or a pair of gold ballet flats. Izogie had been the only one of the four girls who had made an effort during our yoga lessons—the same endurance she showed while learning to read and write. The other girls didn't like the Indian discipline. Not surprisingly. Yoga was taken up by middle-class Westerners in search of enlightenment or the perfect body. But the girls had not undertaken the perilous journey to Europe for spiritual growth, physical dexterity or flat abs. Nevertheless, yoga had seemed a useful tool to shake up the boredom and creeping depression that assaults people damned to sitting around and doing nothing while waiting months or years for the official answer to their asylum request.

Nadia had been the only one of my friends who immediately took me up on it when I asked her to volunteer at the refugee home. We had a game plan. Yoga lessons in English first and later in Italian—that way, the girls could develop their language skills and we could open up the lessons to the women in town, offering something to the villagers too. It would all have sounded great in a leaflet outlining our charity's approach to integration, but yoga didn't turn out to be the new soccer. Kicking a ball on the local pitch was the first, and often only, way for the young African men staying at the shelters in Italy to meet locals. But it didn't work that way with our yoga lessons.

Hope and Joyce had already collapsed onto their pink mats. And Hope was (again!) wearing a pair of skinny jeans and an intricate weave that made any movement impossible. I wasn't looking forward to another chat about suitable gym wear. Nadia told Hope to undo the button of her jeans so that she could breathe properly and asked Joyce to wait to readjust her skewed wig until after class. Pieces of fake hair littered the gym after every lesson. I looked up and put a foot forward to prepare for the next position and saw an exasperated Nadia shaking her head. I wouldn't have been surprised if our yoga teacher was the next person to go missing after downward-facing dog.

***

By the beginning of November, it was obvious that the disappearances of Precious and Fola were no longer just a humanitarian concern for Lesley and me but also a financial one for the charity. The two empty beds meant less funding, and just like a doctor needs enough patients to make a living, a refugee home requires a minimum number of asylum seekers to pay the bills. There were still people arriving in Sicily throughout autumn, but most of them were men. And because of its legacy as a women's shelter, our house couldn't accept any male refugees.

"What do you think will happen?" Lesley asked me.

"I don't have a clue." I was at a loss with the whole situation. Lesley and I still didn't have a contract, nor had we been paid the promised salary. Lesley had received a contract and salary for the month of August, and I had always been paid punctually for my work at the women's shelter in the past. Hence, we both felt the situation would be clarified once Teresa had a bit more time. But things were incredibly slow, even by Italian standards. Lesley and her mum didn't have to pay rent at the refugee home, which helped them manage. But we both kept spending our own money. The extra bottle of shampoo or can of tomato sauce here and there wasn't a big issue, but the gas for trips to the police station and hospital in the city started to add up. As with the contract and salary, Teresa insisted that the expenses would be taken care of as soon as things had started to calm down a bit. I started to wonder, though, when that would be. Teresa never came up to the house and hardly ever answered my phone calls or emails. She had hired me to run the refugee home, and I was happy to organize the job as I saw fit, but there were things I had to decide together with her. She also had to hand me the pocket money for the girls once a month. They needed the 2.50 euros a day to recharge their phones and have a little bit of spending money. However, the pocket money arrived with more delay each month, and the weekly food shopping started to become more frugal from week to week. I had no insight into the financial dealings of the charity, but my main worry wasn't the delayed payments but the realization that we didn't know what we were actually dealing with.

I had not been able to get back in touch with Fola and Precious and couldn't figure out what the other girls were planning to do. Any inquiries from our side were met with a Mafia-like *omertà*. Izogie, Hope and Joyce seemed to live in a parallel world that only narrowly overlapped with the universe I called home. We kept meeting at the intersections and were as much annoyed as amused and entertained by each other. And the more time we spent together, the more it became clear that I didn't have the faintest idea about what was really going on.

10

I called Teresa for an appointment. She didn't answer. I sent
her an email and a text message. She didn't answer. I resent the
email and the text message and tried to call again. Nothing. The
pocket money for the girls had been due for two weeks. They
were complaining, and rightly so. I checked my agenda for the
days Teresa was supposed to be at the town hall and drove there
right away. She was sitting in her new office, hunched over her
laptop, intently studying something on her computer screen. I
said hello. She looked up and seemed surprised to see me.

"Oh, hello." Teresa shuffled some papers and pointed to a
chair.

"I sent you an email," I said, sitting down.

"Ah, yes, I saw it."

"And several text messages."

"Yes, I would have called you in the afternoon." Her phone
rang. She looked at it, pressed a button on its side and turned it
facedown on the table. So this was what happened to my phone
calls.

"How are you?" I asked.

"Oh, fine."

"What's going on? I haven't heard from you about the pocket
money."

"It hasn't arrived yet."

"It hasn't? Again?"

"It looks like we'll have to wait until next week."

"Next week? That won't go down well with the girls. They have already been waiting for it for half of the month."

"I don't think we're asking too much if they have to wait for once until the end of the month."

She had a point. Compared to everything the girls must have been through since they left Nigeria, having to wait an extra week or two for their pocket money didn't seem that terrible. After all, they had a comfortable bed in a warm and lovely house, their bureaucratic matters were taken care of and—supposedly—useful activities were organized for them. Surely service hadn't been quite like this in Tripoli. But they were not dumb, nor were they a group of helpless victims grateful for every bit of attention they could get. Izogie, Joyce and Hope kept talking to some of the Nigerian girls they had met during their trip and who now lived in shelters in other parts of Tuscany. They knew that the pocket money arrived regularly everywhere else. Why not at our house?

"Teresa, what exactly is happening? Why hasn't the money arrived yet? And what about the food shopping becoming less every week? That's not how I remember things from the women's shelter in the countryside!"

"I know, I wish things were different." Teresa closed her laptop and inspected her short fingernails while talking to me. "The charity is in a bad spot. I'm keeping everything together here with my own money. I've spent fifteen thousand euros in the last three months to keep the women's shelter and refugee home running. Groceries, bills, salaries—do you have any idea how high the running cost is of a structure like ours?"

"You are paying the bills with your own money?"

"I did. But I've reached the limit. I've been telling the board of the charity for months that we're sailing towards an abyss. They have to inject some money, or I don't know what we'll do."

"But why? You've been running the women's shelter for years and things always worked well. What's going on?"

"Italy is in a mess. The second half of the year has always been tight financially, since social services always pay with quite a delay. But this year, the money isn't arriving at all. Social services keep sending women in need our way but no longer pay the bills. I'm normally a positive person, but I'm at my wits' end right now. I have no idea what will happen if the economy doesn't start to pick up soon."

"Sounds like we're heading Greece's way—"

"Towards economic collapse?"

"Exactly."

The charity had been founded more than a decade ago, thanks to several substantial donations. A big part of the money was invested in the creation of a women's shelter in the Tuscan countryside. Safe living conditions for women and children running away from domestic violence were scarce, and the problem wasn't getting smaller. Teresa had been in charge of the project from day one, and the charity had always had the reputation of being absolutely sound. But whatever the amount of the initial donations, the women's shelter could only survive if the daily operating costs were covered by the government.

Teresa had opened her laptop and was staring back at her screen. I left the office and went to the bar for a second cappuccino. I took my cup out onto the terrace and watched the light change over the legendary rolling hills. Unbothered by the dire state of the country's economy, the gentle slopes looked as peaceful as ever in the gold-tinted autumn colors—after all, it wasn't the first time that Italy was falling to pieces. But for once, I didn't feel reassured by the comforting view. I had no idea how to help. Unlike Teresa, I didn't have fifteen thousand euros in the bank that I could pull out and distribute among the poor. But even if I had, judging from Teresa's example, her private donation hadn't managed to sort out anything. If the state was running out of money, all the private associations and charities relying on it wouldn't be far behind. And the people who'd feel the crash first were the ones who didn't have much to start with, like the women and children staying at Teresa's shelter. Some of them had been there for years. The idea was to help everybody become self-sufficient as soon as possible, but in the current economy, this was easier said than done. Martina, the Italian teacher at the refugee home, had just moved back to Holland. Her plan had been to return to Italy and settle in the area where she had grown up, but after a summer job in a restaurant that only opened during high season, she couldn't find anything that would have gotten her through the rest of the year. If it was difficult to find a regular job for somebody like Martina—young, flexible and with a degree—it was even worse for a woman with two or three kids to look after.

I paid for my coffee and drove to the refugee home, wondering what to tell the girls. Izogie had to recharge her prepaid phone, and Hope needed money for the train fare to Pisa. She wanted to visit a Nigerian friend, whom she had gotten to know through a Facebook group. I had already told them a week ago that they would have to wait for a few more days and they hadn't been impressed. I passed two elderly hunters in army apparel along the curvy road that lead to Dogana. They were calling and whistling for a dog that must have gotten lost. I was tempted to stop the car and help them with their search. I wasn't a fan of hunting, but I wished I could work on a problem that might have an easy and straightforward solution. I drove on to talk to the girls instead.

"Mum," Izogie called from the shower when I walked up the stairs to the second floor, "you've brought our money, right?"

***

I spent several hours at the house explaining what was happening and trying to figure out what could be done to mitigate the damage. I also talked to Anna and her family. They were in the same boat. In a way, they were even worse off.

"But Teresa told us not to worry about anything," Anna said looking at me in disbelief. "She always said we could stay here as long as we needed to, even though social services don't pay for us."

"Why don't social services pay for you?" The government paid the charity thirty-five euros per refugee per day. From what I knew, a similar amount was compensated for by social services for the women and children who had to leave their homes because of domestic violence.

"We never got the support. Perhaps because my kids are all older than sixteen. And I was so afraid of my husband that I didn't want to accuse him of anything in the beginning. I did in the end, but it didn't change anything. We are totally dependent on the charity until I find a job. Teresa knows I've been doing everything to find a job since I first arrived here. She said not to worry."

"I know."

"If things are so bad, why didn't she tell me?"

"I think Teresa is doing a lot of great things, but she isn't particularly good at telling people when she can't help anymore. Call her and talk to her directly."

"I've been trying to call her all week, but she doesn't answer."

"You're not the only one. Try stalking her at the town hall. That's the only thing that works for me."

"But what about the bus tickets? I need the money to renew them this week. The kids need to get to school. Michele already got fined once. They are no longer allowed on unless they have their tickets!"

The bus fare had been a source of continuous tension. There were no educational options in the countryside. Anna's children all had to travel to the city. They risked a fine if they didn't have a valid ticket, whereas refugees could apply for a cheap one-year travel pass that cost less than Anna's children's monthly student travel card. Joyce, Hope and Precious didn't have their passes yet, but even though some drivers made it clear that they didn't like the system (or really didn't like them, I sometimes suspected), they were always allowed onto the bus and didn't get fined.

"I can help with the money for this month. But in the meantime, we have to come up with something else." I told her that I had decided to charge rent for the gym room. The group of elderly women from the village who used it twice a week hadn't paid any rent for use of the room so far. I had already called the teacher on the drive up to let him know that we needed to charge from now on. He had said he'd have to raise the fee for the course, then. This wouldn't gain me points with the old ladies. Quite a few of them didn't have much of a pension themselves. But it was all I could think of so far, and it would help with the bus tickets.

It was dark when I left Dogana. The phone call from Laura arrived on my drive home to our town. Laura was a social worker whom I had met several times. She organized the first health checkups at the emergency reception center in the city for the refugees arriving from Sicily. We had run into her a couple of weeks ago after Joyce, Hope and Izogie had lodged the papers for the renewal of their first permits of stay. The girls had been very happy to see her. She was lovely and did a great job. I liked her too.

"I'm sorry, I know it's late, but I need to ask you something," Laura said.

"For sure, shoot away. What is it?"

"I received a call from Hope and Joyce. They sounded very upset. They say you don't pay them their pocket money?"

"When did they call you?"

"Just now. What's happening? I can't imagine that it's true that you're not paying their pocket money. But as I said, they sounded very upset, so I thought I better check with you to see what's going on. You *do* give them their money, don't you?"

I asked Laura to hang on for a moment and pulled over to park on a dirt track leading to an olive grove. I wished I had a cigarette. I was not much of a smoker, but being accused of swindling a group of Nigerian refugees out of their pocket money called for a smoke and a double whiskey.

I drove home half an hour later and told Sergio what had happened. He was preparing dinner and interrupted the stirring of the pasta sauce with fits of swearing about ungrateful immigrants, useless social workers, me being a fool, Italy being a nightmare, Italian politicians being even worse, and so on. But he was most pissed off with the girls.

"Calling somebody to check on you? After all you've been doing for them?"

I was disappointed too. Hurt, actually. Here I was, running around for everybody like a madwoman and the first thing they did once something didn't work out as promised was phone around to complain, while probably making the call from the phone that I had given them! But rather than feeling sorry for myself, I had to figure out why I was expecting the girls to trust me blindly. Considering Italy had seen quite a few scandals of refugee homes being set up by dubious associations not to help but to make some quick and easy money, it was only good for them if they knew what to do if they had reason to doubt the charity's seriousness. During all our conversations about human trafficking and prostitution, Lesley and I had kept telling them never to believe anybody, especially if the person kept making promises without delivering the goods. Trust was such a fragile currency. Hope had been sold by her own aunt. Bags of Swiss chocolate and the extra hours I put in didn't mean I could be trusted not to rip them off.

***

I drove to the town hall first thing in the morning. I had promised Lesley that I'd call her afterward. We had had a long talk. Lesley needed the job much more than I did, but we both agreed that this wasn't working. I had not even tried to call Teresa for an appointment. I knew she wouldn't answer. She was in a meeting with the mayor when I arrived. I knocked at the door and asked whether she had a moment.

"I can't, we need at least another hour here."

I went outside to wait in the sunshine in the piazza. It was market day. I chatted with some of the old ladies who were shopping at the stalls and bought some oranges and tangerines. Fresh fruit was the thing the girls missed most in the dwindling food shopping every week. I got back to the town hall an hour later. Teresa was in her office putting on her coat.

"Hi, again."

"Oh, I have to run off," Teresa said.

"I can see that, but I only need ten minutes."

"Okay, what is it?" Teresa sat down without taking off her coat.

"I've talked to Lesley. We can't keep going on like this."

"I don't think I understand. Keep going on like what?"

"The situation at the refugee home: the lack of money, the shopping—it's putting a lot of strain on everybody. From what we hear, other refugee homes don't have the financial issues we have. Let's find another home for the girls. There are several in Tuscany where they have friends, and some of them might have free spaces. Unless we have a stable setup, this won't work."

"Ah, no, don't worry, I got it all sorted."

"Sorry?"

"We've sorted it out. I'll be able to give you the pocket money this week. The bank is giving us some credit until the new organization steps in."

"The new organization?"

"Yes, they will take over by the end of the year."

"Great, and thanks for telling me. Useful to know, since I actually work for you!"

"I was going to tell you but haven't had the time yet." Teresa grabbed her bag and stood up. "I've been under a lot of pressure. The women's shelter has been my baby for the last ten years. I couldn't just let the ship sink like this. Plus, all the other refugee homes in Tuscany are full. It would be impossible to find any free beds for the girls."

"I'm not sure—"

"I really have to go now. Next time!" Teresa opened the door and left me staring at the empty wall in her office.

I was starting to take this personally. I could see that Teresa was in a difficult position, but shutting down communication wasn't the way forward. When had she been planning to tell me that a new organization was taking over? And *which* organization? I jumped up and ran after her.

"Oh, it's the charity you already know. The one that runs the emergency reception center in the city. They have lots of experience. They'll do a great job."

III

WINTER

11

Casanova staggered down the wide and mossy steps of the crumbling Tuscan countryside mansion. He was in a great mood, even though his powdered wig and embroidered cloak must have seen better times. He crossed to the other side of the garden and joined a small group of peculiarly dressed people who were staring into the flames of a bonfire. A joint made its round, and a pale nun topped up the wine glasses. The clear December night was chilly but not yet cold. Casanova grabbed a long iron fork and moved a few pieces of burning wood out of the fire—a crate of sausages needed to be barbecued for his eccentric guests.

Sergio was looking uncomfortable under his synthetic wig. I grabbed his arm and mouthed, "Can we go home?"

He didn't hear me, his attention absorbed by the striking décolletage and teasing chatter of a woman I couldn't recognize behind her Venetian mask. I left them to it, walked off and ran into an old friend who was wearing a pearl-trimmed corset and a long puffed-up silk gown that would have looked perfectly at home on the stage of the Royal Opera House.

"Darling, how are you?"

"I'm great!" I wasn't well at all and hoped to avoid a long conversation.

"So lovely to see you. It has been ages. What have you been up to? Ah, it's a shame we never have time to catch up!"

"I'm still working at the refugee home. In fact, I wanted to contact you about—"

"Oh yes, your emails, I remember. I'm *so* sorry, but I didn't have a *single* moment yet to look through our books and clothes. It's just been *crazy*. Work, the kids, you know how it is. We're all *so* busy! But yes, absolutely, the *next* time I manage to find a free moment. But you *must* tell me, how are you? I've seen it on the news. It must be terrible, all these *poor* people. But *what* can we do?"

I was about to launch into a long tirade explaining, that actually, there *were* lots of things that *we* could do when a gentleman in a pitch-black velvet suit and two very prominent front teeth interrupted us. Dracula? Wasn't he at the wrong party?

"Exquisite dress, my dear." He fingered the lace on the hem of my friend's dress and planted an exaggerated kiss on her gloved hand.

"Oh, do you like it? I sewed it myself. Half a week of research and half a week of work just to look good tonight!" She raised her skirt a bit and giggled. "And look what I've found to wear underneath! I had to drive *all* the way to Florence to—" I seized the opportunity to duck down and get out of the conversation while the count bent over to inspect her vintage hosiery.

I took a stroll around the timeworn house and found an empty room with a couple of sofas lined up and a movie running on the opposite wall. *Fellini's Casanova* was being screened on an old bedsheet, a fitting setup if there ever was one. The movie was on mute, and a lonesome guest danced—red wine bottle in one hand and half-full glass in the other—to the thumping electronic beats that arrived from the room next door. A vain-and arrogant-looking Donald Sutherland pulled out his bag of tricks to seduce a young woman. I watched the baroque lovemaking on the screen and the out-of-rhythm moves of the drunk dancer in front of it and thought of the refugee home.

I had been there in the afternoon to deliver the pocket money that had finally arrived. The atmosphere in the house was at a low point. Anna and her kids were despairing; they still had not found jobs. They hid in front of the TV, which was always on. Joyce and Izogie seemed listless and depressed. Spending much time indoors since the temperatures had dropped didn't help. Hope was the only one who kept her spirits up, since she couldn't wait to visit her friend in Pisa. I had had a meeting with the core team of the new organization. Pio, the boss, and Maria and Domenico, two social workers I had already met at a couple of meetings in the city. They seemed professional and like a good team. I was looking forward to working with them starting in the new year. But I was tired from the whole disorganization and lack of structure and support we had to deal with until then, and I was worried about the Italian economy, the ever-growing rate of unemployment and the fate of the people residing at our refugee home.

Casanova was in Rome now. The dancer had collapsed on the sofa next to me, hugging the empty red wine bottle on his chest. I tried to give the movie a second chance but still didn't like it. It seemed like a mirror image of the world around me, which distorted my friends' frivolous party into a hollow and decadent eccentricity that resembled life at the court of Louis XVI at the dawn of the French Revolution.

***

I woke up late on Sunday morning. The kids were still at Sergio's parents'. He made a cappuccino for me and an espresso for himself. He put coffee and newspapers on a tray and took them down to the table in our olive grove. The early-December sun was surprisingly strong. Sergio went back up to the house to get us two hats, while I leafed through the Saturday newspaper. It looked like Italy wanted to remind me of its bright side. Winter days spent soaking up the sun was one of the reasons I had moved here in the first place.

"Feeling better?" Sergio said, back with his Panama hat on and a crumpled straw hat in hand for me.

"I don't know. Just remind me not to come along to another costume party. They really don't work for me."

"At least there was enough food." I knew what he was trying to do. This was Sergio hoping to make me laugh by shifting my attention to something that kept driving *him* crazy about my international group of friends. The first time we attended a party together, we had arrived hungry but a little late and found that the buffet had already been completely eaten up. Sergio had remained so deeply traumatized by the night our dinner consisted of a single leftover piece of cake that he wouldn't accept an invitation by any of my British, Swiss or American friends without mentioning beforehand that we better pack some sandwiches. He obviously never worried about it when we were invited by Italians. But I wasn't in the mood to defend my non-Italian friends and engage in our usual debate about Italy against the rest of the world.

"I just think it's absurd that everybody is so fucking occupied with their children, incredible careers and ailing pets and parents, but—surprise!—not too busy to play Venice reborn on top of a Tuscan hill."

"Nobody is perfect."

"I know. I'm just tired and overreacting. But it looks like the world is going to pieces and nobody cares. And if Italy is going the way of Greece, the people hit hardest won't be the ones who spend their Saturday nights playing hide-and-seek under rococo gowns." Our cat jumped onto the table, circling my cappuccino. I tried to shoo her away and get over my anger. "I guess I just need a break. No worrying about food shopping, paying for bus tickets and girls disappearing into a black hole, while the world around me is busy ordering powdered wigs from eBay."

Sergio nodded supportively.

"Let's go on a holiday once they pay me."

"You still think they'll pay you?" Sergio laughed, and touched the brim of his hat with his index and middle fingers in a "so long" gesture. "I wouldn't count on it."

"I know they will. They've always paid me. Why shouldn't they, once they've worked out their financial mess?"

"*Povera illusa!*"

"Right, I may be naïve and too trusting, but really, that's not it. This whole thing just shows how unfair everything is and how little we do about it. We are all so damn spoiled and caught up in our oh-so-busy lives! It just makes me miserable..." Sergio grumbled something and stifled a yawn. "It's like—remember how one feels at fifteen or so, when you realize that the world is an unfair place and nobody cares?"

"Me? I thought the world was a fabulous place when I was fifteen. All those afternoons spent running after a soccer ball!"

"Okay, but when you weren't playing soccer. Didn't you have that kind of awakening? And the guilt and depression that goes with realizing how privileged you are. And that these privileges are built on other people's misery. We look back on centuries of European cruelty, and the few who tried to remedy it were a handful of priests and nuns, who only did all that charitable work as a pretext to infuse every corner of this planet with their world views!"

"Hm," Sergio stroked the back of our purring cat, which insisted on lying on the table, "I guess I was too busy chasing girls, when I wasn't playing soccer."

He stood up, put the cups on the tray and carried it back inside. I poured myself a glass of water and started to leaf through the articles I had printed out during the last months. They all focused on the connection of human trafficking to prostitution. Some proposed that the abolition of prostitution according to the Swedish model was likely to stop the problem. Others asked for decriminalization—a more liberal approach, often put forward by international sex workers' associations—instead of trying to legally stop a demand that, similar to drug use, wouldn't end because of prohibition but just be driven underground. I thought of Casanova and his guests. Instead of running off, I should have asked them for their expert advice.

12

I had taken Joyce, Hope and Izogie along with me to my other job as a travel writer focusing on Tuscany. We had an appointment for a tasting at a Brunello winery in Montalcino. Winter was the perfect season to visit winemakers; with nature asleep, the vignerons had time for a proper chat and thorough tasting without the worry of neglecting their vineyards. The girls were in need of a change of scenery, and I wanted to show them more of the Italian region they had been living in for nearly six months. We stopped at the Sant'Antimo abbey on the way to the winery and had my favorite Romanesque building all to ourselves—another nice thing about winter in Tuscany. The custodian in the church observed us for a while and then pulled out his clarinet for a little impromptu concert. The girls took some photos of the surprise musician before they sat down to pray. I waited in the back pew and enjoyed the different setup. For once, our little group just looked like a bunch of tourists having a good time. Three stylish young Nigerian women—oil money? Nollywood stars?—and the English-speaking Swiss guide they had hired to drive them to Italy's most exclusive wine town. Nigeria's rich and beautiful loved champagne; it made sense that they'd also take to Brunello.

My phone started to ring. The call came from a number I didn't recognize. Joyce turned around and hushed me before I was able to mute it. "We're in a church!"

I went outside to return the call. It was Domenico from the new charity. He told me that they urgently needed to find a place for one of the young Nigerian women staying at their refugee home. She had split up with her boyfriend, who was Nigerian too. He had turned violent and had been thrown out of the project. Now they quickly needed a safe place for her to stay; somewhere he couldn't find her.

"We've got a free bed. But we're in Montalcino right now."

"No problem, we still have to do a couple of things here. I'll call you as soon as we're ready to leave."

Izogie had joined me outside. I asked her to call Joyce and Hope; we had to speed things up.

"Why, mum?"

"Just call them. I'll explain in the car."

The Brunello winery I had chosen for our tasting was located in a striking setting. We stood on its terrace at the end of the visit to take some pictures of the panoramic view. It stretched from the hills of the Val d'Orcia, a UNESCO heritage site, all the way to the Maremma—a part of Tuscany that didn't have a pedigree yet but was nevertheless my favorite. I pointed to the five-star hotel farther down in the valley and mentioned the names of the celebrities who had holidayed there. The girls didn't know any of them. I was getting old.

"Mum, people seriously pay three hundred euros a night to stay there?" Joyce asked.

"Three hundred euros a night per person. For one of the simpler rooms, yes."

Hope laughed. "We should open a hotel in Dogana. It looks just like this!"

"The tourists would definitely appreciate Dogana more than you do."

"Ah, mum, you're always criticizing us!"

"For a reason!"

"Hope is right, mum," Joyce said over her shoulder while snapping a few more pictures, "you're never happy with us. You're always telling us, do this, do that—"

"And," Izogie couldn't wait to jump on the bandwagon, "*don't* do this, and *don't* do that!"

"Whatever we do is wrong." Joyce had turned around and stood, hands on her hips, to land the final blow. "We couldn't do anything right for you, even if we *tried* to!"

"But that's exactly the point. You don't even *try!*" I was prepared for this discussion. I went through the exact same argument several times a day at home with my kids. "All you do is play with your phones. You started off well with the Italian lessons, but in the meantime—when's the last time I've seen any of you open a book to do your homework?"

"Mum, you're repeating yourself."

"I just wish you would take things a bit more seriously. You are stuck here. We don't have a clue when you'll finally have the appointment for the hearing with the human rights commission in Florence. All we know is that things are terribly slow because of the increasing arrivals in Sicily and the lack of qualified staff at the commission. It's boring and depressing. But since you have to sit here and wait—"

"Mum, you said we have to hurry!" The girls had heard my sermon before and started to walk back to the car.

But I had wanted to show them Montalcino for a reason. More and more of the manual labour in the famous Sangiovese vineyards was done by workers from Morocco and Turkey, and some arrived from as far away as Bangladesh or Pakistan. These jobs were hard physical work. Izogie had grown up in the countryside and might be able to manage, but I couldn't see Hope or Joyce surviving out in the field for more than a day. I knew what I was talking about—I had romanticized a life in agriculture when settling in Tuscany but had given up on the idea for good after six continuous weeks of olive picking. The hospitality industry, however, was a different matter, and it was one of the few sectors in Italy's ailing economy that wasn't stalling. Hotels serving a mainly Italian clientele had been lamenting dwindling numbers for years, but not the ones that catered to wealthy tourists from abroad. Hope and Joyce lacked work experience, but they spoke English, something a lot of Italians—even young ones looking for a job—were still not very good at. I had mentioned my idea to create placements for work experience in the tourism industry for English-speaking refugees to an American journalist whose husband ran a hotel in the Val d'Orcia. She was interested in doing some brainstorming and had promised to contact me once she got back to Italy before the start of the season in March. I had talked the idea through with the girls too. Hope seemed excited about it on some days. On others—especially when I pestered her to study more—she laughed and insisted all she needed was a rich man. No doubt a hotel lounge wasn't the worst place to start.

From the winery we drove on to a friend's place who had invited us for lunch. Raffaella lived with her family in an old Tuscan stone house tucked away in the woods near Montalcino. Chickens scurried through the terraced garden when we arrived, and a couple of cats slept in the sun. All it took to forget Italy's financial crisis, political disasters and any worries about the dire state of the world was half an hour under the pergola in this garden with a glass of red wine and a few antipasti. Raffaella had fired up the wood stove, a big pot of jollof rice was sitting on it

110

and various side dishes were already laid out on the table. I was relieved to see her choice of menu. I would have felt embarrassed if three plates of handmade gnocchi had been left untouched by the end of our lunch.

"You know how to prepare jollof rice?" Hope asked.

Raffaella laughed. "It's an experiment. I had to ask Google for help."

The girls didn't look worried and immediately started to fill their plates. I told them to stop, since we were still waiting for Raffaella's husband to join us, when my phone rang. Domenico and Rita, our new Nigerian guest, were nearly ready to leave. I withdrew my orders and filled a plate myself.

"Let's eat, we need to hurry."

We ate as much as we could and rushed out twenty minutes later. I drove back up the dirt road, where we met the approaching car of Raffaella's husband. He pulled to the side to make space for my car to pass on the narrow road. I waved and he returned my greeting, looking startled to see his lunch party speeding off.

"Mum, your friend, what's her name? She's a very good cook." Hope said, while connecting her phone to the stereo in the car. "That jollof rice tasted great."

"You should have told her yourself. What better way to practice your Italian?"

"See, mum," Joyce chipped in from the back, "you are already criticizing again."

I had eaten too much too quickly and, for once, couldn't be bothered to retort. I gave a sketchy lecture about Montalcino's history instead, focusing on the town's century-long rivalry with Siena until the two enemies joined forces against an overpowering Florence.

Hope clicked the music player on her phone and any further communication became impossible. The voice of Ice Prince, one of Nigeria's best-known rap and hip hop artists filled my car.

"That spend a lot of cash oh," Izogie and Joyce sang along with him.

"That spend a lot of cash oh," Hope joined in.

Ice Prince's lyrics perfectly fit the area we were driving through. People did indeed spend a lot of cash-oh in Montalcino.

Izogie reached out from the back seat to turn the volume of the stereo to the maximum. I rolled my window down and sang along to the refrain.

"It's my guy. It's my guy." And again, "It's my guy," since this was all I could understand.

The wind blew our muddled backup chorus through the Tuscan idyll. Cypress trees bent down to see what we were up to. Gnarly olive trees shook their booty, thankful for the different beat after centuries of the same old tune. Hope kept pressing repeat, and we started afresh. Vineyard workers looked up from the vines they were trimming to watch our rolling sound machine boom through the valley. Life wasn't too bad as the driver of three Nigerian movie stars. They were fun to work for. A bit bossy but definitely fun.

***

Back at the refugee home, it was my turn to be bossy again.

"Joyce, please sweep the floor. And Hope, have a look at the bathrooms."

"Mum, we cleaned the whole house two days ago. You know Lesley, she won't leave until she's scrubbed the whole kitchen with us."

"Nobody cleaned before we arrived," Izogie said. She was putting new sheets on the second bed in her room. Precious had slept in it and it looked like it hadn't been changed since she had left.

"Anna cleaned before you arrived, so it seems only nice if you do the same for Rita."

"Who is Rita?"

"The girl arriving now. You might have met her."

"No, mum. There was no Rita on the boat with us."

I opened the nightstand next to Precious's former bed and found a few used tissues, a pair of earrings I had brought along for the *Odyssey* party in August and a ripped-open bar of Toblerone. Only half a piece of the chocolate Matterhorn had been bitten off. She obviously hadn't liked it.

The doorbell rang. We opened the window and saw Domenico and Rita standing in front of the car. Rita wore a pink blazer and skirt and Jackie Kennedy sunglasses. Domenico signaled for us to come down to the car; they needed help. *With what?* I wondered.

I presented myself to Rita while Domenico opened the trunk of the car. Their charity's multipurpose van was packed with suitcases and bags of every size, form and shape.

"How long has Rita been staying with you?" I asked.

"Nine months."

I couldn't believe how much stuff she had. We hauled the first load up the bumpy medieval stairs and went back down for more. There was an elevator in the house, but it didn't work and there was no money to repair it. We stacked the bags in the hallway. The house had been restored with care, and the girls shared lovely double and triple rooms with a bathroom each. But the rooms were small and the wardrobes in them even smaller.

I asked the girls to show Rita the house. And the attic. Maybe some of her stuff could be stored under the roof. They started the tour, and I took advantage of being able to talk to Domenico in person.

"How is the take-over coming along?"

"We're on it. We're preparing the paper work this month. We're not going to make it before Christmas, with the holiday and all. But we'll be ready to step in at the beginning of January."

"We can't wait. Things are really not working here."

"Don't worry, we'll sort it out. We've got years of experience running refugee homes."

Domenico rolled a cigarette. I accompanied him back down to the car. A forlorn sandal with silver straps was still lying in its trunk. Domenico handed it to me, promised to send Rita's paper work via email the following week and told me to call if we had any problems. I went back inside to properly welcome Rita, who was already waiting for me by the door.

"Did the girls show you everything in the house?"

"Yes, mum."

"Any questions you have, just ask me or the girls, and then there is Lesley too and her mum."

"Yes, they told me. They are from the same part of Nigeria as I."

Rita was Igbo, had grown up in a village in Delta State in southern Nigeria and moved to Lagos as a teenager. She had been in Italy for nine months but didn't seem to speak any Italian yet.

"Have you already met the Italians in the house? They don't speak a lot of English, but you can ask them too. Anna's son is really nice and a good cook." The girls were always surprised to see Michele do most of the cooking for his family. I put on my coat and got ready to leave.

"Mum, how can I get to the train station in the city? I have to be in Rome tomorrow."

"The buses to town run three or four times a day. The girls know the timetable—just ask them. But I think it is best you take some time to sort out your bags and suitcases first. We can see about Rome next week."

"Mum, I have to go tomorrow. It's my brother's wedding."

"You have a brother who lives in Rome?"

"Yes, with his wife and their two children."

"With his wife? Didn't you just say he is getting married tomorrow?"

"At the town hall, yes. They married years ago but only at the church."

I looked for the printout with the bus timetable but couldn't find it. "I think the first bus leaves at six thirty in the morning. It will take an hour to get to the city. We're farther away from civilization here than you were in the old refugee home."

"Don't worry, mum. As long as there is a bus, I'll be fine."

"Ask one of the girls to show you where the bus stop is. There is a timetable there too, but they probably know all the connections by heart."

"Thanks." Rita turned around and walked up the stairs. Her tight pink skirt stretched to the edges with every step she took.

"Oh, wait, your sandal!"

"Mum?" She stopped and looked down.

I held her sandal up by its silver straps.

"Ah, this one. I don't know where the other one is. You can throw it away." Jackie Kennedy went upstairs.

I shook my head and did as she told me.

***

I called the girls on Saturday morning. Yes, Rita had left on the first bus. She called me on Sunday to confirm that she would be back on Monday. I had to send a daily email to the police, which indicated who was present at the house and who wasn't. The girls had started to travel a lot, and their mood was a lot better each time they had spent a few days in Florence, Rome or Pisa. But although traveling helped ameliorate their creeping dejection, it didn't do any good for the refugee home's disastrous finances. The government only paid the charity the thirty-five euros per refugee per day on the days the refugees actually stayed overnight. This made sense from the government's point of view, but it made the situation tricky for the homes, which had to remind their inhabitants not to travel and visit friends in other parts of Italy too often. Otherwise, the home risked losing out on too much money, which would endanger the whole project. Our own home was the perfect example that things were doomed to fail financially unless a minimum number of people was present (and hence paid for) daily. However, going to the city to meet new people and network was a proactive approach for refugees staying at the homes in the countryside. They were making connections for a future that we hoped was going to be independent of government subsidies. Many refugee homes had popped up in the Italian countryside, but most people staying at them would move to the cities sooner or later. The depressed economy in the Italian hinterland didn't offer many job opportunities.

I went back to the refugee home on Tuesday morning. I had to bring up an old laptop and iMac friends had sent me from Switzerland, as I wanted to teach the girls computer skills. I had planned to download a free program for speed typing, but it didn't work on the Mac. And the menu on the laptop kept switching back to German. I had tried to change the language on the computer several times to download free word processing and spreadsheet programs. The girls were better with their smartphones than I was, so I expected them to be quick on the uptake with computers too, but OpenOffice in German wouldn't help. The shaky computer hardware was about to turn one more of my lofty projects into a failure. It was nothing new. I kept planning useful activities that were supposed to support the girls' education and integration but ended up spending most of my time rewriting shopping lists and house cleaning schedules nobody paid attention to anyway. I also spent entire mornings on the phone trying to convince technicians to come by to fix broken washing machines and leaking water heaters, even though their last bills hadn't been paid yet. The sewing machine and boxes of material a friend had given me for hands-on intercultural activities with the elderly women in the village stood in a corner collecting dust, and the computers would soon join them. I was too busy discussing with the operators of the women's shelter—which had to do the shopping for the two houses with less and less money—whether we truly needed two extra packets of rice and another three cans of tomato sauce each week. I kept telling the girls to use less soap and shampoo when they showered and had to remind Anna and her family that fabric softener and cotton swabs didn't belong on a shopping list at times like these. The intercultural mediation I had supposedly been hired for had turned me into a sort of Stasi officer who contemplated installing cameras in the bathrooms to prove that the girls used far more generous portions of toothpaste and body lotion than they said they did. And was body lotion an indispensable item in a refugee home? I didn't think so but had to reconsider each time Hope or Izogie showed me their dry and cracked skin.

Vera was the only one up when I arrived at the house with my computers. She was looking frail and sad in her double layer of pajamas and padded dressing gown. I asked for news of her grandchildren, and she just shook her head and sighed. I knew that Lesley had met with her lawyer after visiting the kids at the beginning of the week, but it looked like she hadn't received positive news. Vera wrapped herself tighter into her robe. It had gotten cold, but for the moment the gas heating was still working. I wondered for how long. Vera put the coffee on and asked whether I wanted a piece of cake.

"Cake? Oh wow, who made a cake?"

"Rita brought it along from Rome." Vera opened the fridge and cut off a slice from the remains of a cake that was richly decorated in white and pink.

"Seriously, she brought this home? On the train from Rome?" I picked the colored marzipan flowers off, took a bite of the spongy cake and realized that I hadn't believed for a moment that Rita had indeed attended a wedding in Rome.

13

A couple of days before Christmas, we were back at the immigration office to lodge the request for the renewal of the girls' permits of stay. It was the third renewal since their arrival in Italy in July. After two permits for three months each, their new *permessi di soggiorno* were going to be valid for a full six months. And they were also supposed to have a work permit to go with them, even though Izogie, Hope and Joyce still hadn't received the appointment for their hearing at the human rights commission in Florence.

We were by now regulars at the immigration office and drove to a Chinese shop in the town center once the paper work was done. Rita had told the girls about the good deals at the shop, and I agreed to stop there since it was one of my favorites too. I dropped the girls in front of the shop, parked the car and searched my handbag for the Christmas presents list. I had to find last-minute gifts for various members of my family and everybody at the house in Dogana. Izogie and Rita were haggling with the young Chinese woman behind the cash register when I entered the shop. Izogie wanted two pairs of sunglasses for the price of one, and Rita was undecided between several smartphone covers. I chose a pair of glittery leggings for each of the girls and found a few loud and useless battery-devouring gadgets for my kids that represented the exact opposite of the wooden-toy-only principles of my Swiss parenting. I paid the friendly shop assistant and pointed to the pile of bags, junk jewelry and synthetic clothes that the girls had amassed on the counter.

"I'm sorry," I said, "we're creating quite a lot of work for you."

"Don't worry," the young woman pulled out a stack of red plastic bags with Chinese characters printed on them, "they are buying all of it."

"They are buying all of it?" Eighty euros of monthly pocket money didn't seem to allow for shopping sprees like this.

Hope joined me at the counter with a fake silver necklace with a Hello Kitty pendant. "Do you like this, mum?"

"It's cute." Hope held the necklace up to my chest.

"Would you wear it?"

"That's sweet, love, but I don't think my daughter would be very excited if I started to wear Hello Kitty too."

"Oh, right, it's a perfect Christmas present for her, then." Hope put the necklace on one of the piles on the counter and asked for the bill. "And I'll get something for Sergio and my future husband too!"

"I don't think my son is quite going to be the rich husband you're looking for." Hope had always enjoyed meeting my family and kept teasing my son by saying that she wanted to marry him the day he'd turn eighteen.

"Don't worry, mum, I'll be rich myself by then." Hope pulled out two fifty-euro bills from her purse, and I wondered whether my family's Christmas presents were just being paid for with the rewards of the oldest profession in the world.

Back in the car, I was about to address the issue of their surprising financial resources when Izogie told me to drop her at the station.

"At the station? Why?"

"I'm going to Florence."

"You're going to Florence? Today?"

"Yes, mum. I'll stay with friends 'til after Christmas."

I wasn't quite ready for this. I had gotten used to Hope, Joyce and Rita traveling, but Izogie had always stayed at the house. I felt disappointed that she wouldn't be around for our Christmas party.

"You're sure you want to leave today? Can't it wait 'til after Christmas?"

"No, mum, I'm going now."

"But you don't even have a jacket." Izogie had left the house in the morning without one and I hadn't intervened. It was a warm December day, and I had expected us to be back in the early afternoon.

"Mum, I'll be fine."

I agreed to drive her to the station and explained that she had to change trains to get to Florence. The bus would have been easier, since it was cheaper and quicker, but she insisted she wanted to go by train.

"Have you ever been on a train before?"

"No, I haven't."

"But how will you know where you have to get off?" Izogie had learned to read simple words in our textbook, but I doubted she could decipher the name of an Italian station from a rolling train, especially if she had never heard it in the first place.

"Mum, she'll ask." Rita was leaning forward into the space between the two front seats. "It's impossible to get lost in Italy. You just call somebody and ask for help." Rita held her two phones up and seemed amused that this hadn't occurred to me yet.

"So this is why you're always on the phone?" I had hardly

finished the phrase when one of the two started ringing. Rita sat back to answer it. I watched her in the rearview mirror. She looked like a cranky hip hop artist with her shaved head (the Jackie Kennedy outfit was for showtime only). But it seemed she had a parallel life as a busy operator connecting lost Nigerians all over Italy with their fellow citizens who had come through the same train station or bus stop before. I imagined her future as the living alternative to Google Maps, with headquarters located right at our refugee home. No doubt, Dogana could do with a forward-thinking business venture. And we already had the free lunchtime yoga classes for the stressed-out employees.

"Don't worry, mum. I'll be fine," Izogie said.

I had parked at the station, and Izogie got out of the car. She was right. Illiterate or not, somebody who had survived a year in war-torn Tripoli could handle a train ride in Italy. I watched her walk to the entrance of the station. She looked lovely, in a neat pair of blue jeans and a crisp white shirt, but not like somebody who was going on a trip for a weekend. Izogie had her phone and a small purse, which seemed to be all she needed. She turned around, waved and laughed before she disappeared among the people in front of the station. Hope opened the door to sit in the front with me.

"Do you think she'll come back?" I couldn't let it go.

"Mum!" The girls rolled their eyes.

I started the car and drove them back to Dogana to the chatter of pidgin and continuously ringing phones.

***

We celebrated our Christmas party on the evening of the twenty-fifth. The residents at the house were all Christian. Anna and her family were hard-core Catholics, and from what I understood, the Nigerians, including Lesley and Vera, belonged to various Pentecostal churches. But Anna and her children weren't around. Anna had sent me a message a few days earlier to tell me that they had been invited to celebrate Christmas Eve with friends. When I replied that we could easily celebrate on the evening of the twenty-fifth instead, she answered that her friends had invited them to stay over for that night too. I had a feeling it was an excuse, but I couldn't blame them.

Sergio, the kids and I arrived in the early evening on Christmas Day. A nice spicy scent welcomed us. Hope was squatting in the kitchen in front of a big aluminium pot. It was easier to stir the semolina fufu like this. The doughlike dish was one of my favorites. The fufu was formed into little balls right at the table, and then dipped by hand into a peppery soup or sauce. The other girls came downstairs to help with the preparations in the kitchen. Hope, Rita and Joyce all had a layer of something grayish on their faces, and their weaves and braided extensions were held back by hairnets and towels.

"What do you have on your face?"

"It's a beauty treatment. It cleans the skin."

"I know facial masks, but why do you have them on now?"

"We saw Anna's son use it. We just put it on. He says it works best if you leave it on for at least an hour."

The girls set the table, and we all sat down for our Christmas dinner. Lesley was visiting her kids at the children's home. Her mum sat next to me and from time to time reached over to squeeze my hand. Her grandchildren had been picked up at the women's shelter by the police more than a year ago. And she still hadn't been allowed to visit them at the children's home. It was ridiculous and surely not for the benefit of the kids, who had spent a big part of their time at home with their grandmother, who looked after them when Lesley was at work. I looked around the table and was sorry Anna and her kids weren't here. I had wanted to at least once have everybody sitting around the same table. Joyce turned up the speakers on Rita's phone: Harrysong's "Beta Pikin" was our "Silent Night." Its refrain had accompanied us on many of our car rides.

"Have you heard from Izogie?"

The three ghostlike faces on the other side of the table shook their heads. The girls' appearance was surreal, but in line with the rest of the month. Sergio and I had started December with a group of people in Venetian masks reenacting the time of Casanova on a Tuscan hill. It was only natural that we'd end up spending Christmas night sharing fufu and my mother-in-law's homemade lasagna with the cast from Michael Jackson's "Thriller" video.

Vera prepared coffee, and I put the presents for Anna and her kids under the fake Christmas tree before we left.

Izogie called when we were on our way back home.

"Mum, I just wanted to say Happy Christmas."

"Are you okay?"

"Yes, mum, it's great to be out of the house. I feel a lot better. I'll be back tomorrow."

"How did the trip go?"

"It took forever. I got off at the wrong station twice. But I got there in the end."

***

As promised on the phone, Izogie returned the day after Christmas. The other girls left three days later to celebrate New Year's Eve in the city. Visiting friends, they said. Friends they seemed to know from back home, their time in Libya or

Facebook since their arrival in Italy. I never found out what exactly went on when they went to Florence, Pisa or Rome. And I wondered about the exact nature of these friendships.

After her trip to Florence, Izogie asked where she could exchange seven hundred Czech korunas. She showed me two bills of the foreign currency and repeated that she had found them in a bag a friend had given her for Christmas. I checked the exchange rate. Izogie's Czech korunas added up to the equivalent of twenty-five euros. And twenty-five euros was the current price a Czech tourist would have had to pay for a merry roadside shag on Christmas night in Florence.

***

Lesley and I had been waiting for news from the charity since the start of January. We knew it might take some time. Italy's holiday season lasted until January 6, and the offices that hadn't closed down were nevertheless operating at a much slower pace. But by January 12 we still hadn't heard from Pio and his team. I sent Domenico an email asking for an appointment with him and his boss, and called Pio and Maria after not hearing back from Domenico. They didn't pick up their phones, and they didn't call back. I didn't even bother to get in touch with Teresa—I knew she wouldn't answer—but I couldn't believe that the people who promised to sort out this mess were already behaving just like her.

After waiting for a reply from any of them for more than twenty-four hours, I sent Pio a text message telling him that Lesley and I had spent six months working without a regular contract and without being paid, and I had no intention of staying on if they thought the absence of communication Teresa had introduced was the way forward. Maria called me shortly after. She told me they were extremely sorry, but things had been totally crazy on their side since the start of the year. They had had several emergencies at the other refugee home and the take-over of the organization turned out to be much more complicated than Pio and Domenico could have possibly foreseen. I explained that I understood their difficult situation, but I had zero tolerance for another round of non-communication.

I was sitting with Hope and Lesley in a doctor's office in the city when I took Maria's call. Hope was feeling sick and weak again and needed a proper checkup with a gynecologist. Maria happened to be nearby and came straight to the clinic to talk to Lesley and me in person. It was good to see her. She was extremely friendly and excused herself at length for not having been able to meet us earlier.

"Pio told me to tell you that things have been difficult, but they're trying to get things moving as quickly as possible."

"But what exactly is happening? Why is it taking so long?" I asked.

Maria shook her head and threw her hands wide apart in the animated and dramatic gesturing of southern Italians. She was from Lecce, the beautiful baroque town in the country's heel, and her piercing blue eyes and blonde hair bore testimony to the Mediterranean's rich past. The easy navigability of the ancient sea bordered by three continents had fostered the exchange not only of goods and culture but also of DNA.

"I don't know the details, but from what Pio told me, it should all be sorted out by the end of February."

Lesley and I looked at each other.

"By the end of February?" Lesley asked. "So what are we supposed to do 'til then?"

126

"I can't say. Sadly, there is nothing we can do until our organization has officially taken over the projects of your charity. We've already met the operators at the women's shelter in the countryside. They are in the same situation as you are up in the townhouse."

"It's not quite the same situation. The operators at the women's shelter at least have a proper contract."

"You don't have a contract? That's normal, though, for volunteers."

I sensed a blast rising in my veins and only managed to keep my voice down out of respect for the setting in which our conversation was taking place. "It's just that we're not volunteers. We had been promised a proper contract six months ago but still haven't received one."

"But why do you keep working like this?"

"Actually, we don't. We told Teresa in November that things couldn't go on like this. I had a lot of respect for her work, but the situation was already absurd in autumn. I told her that we needed to transfer the girls to a different home." The whole waiting room was following our heated discussion by now. "But Teresa said she had already found a solution with you taking over by the end of the year. And now you are arriving here to tell us that your organization will be moving in only by the end of February?"

"Okay. I got it. That sucks. But why has Teresa not provided your contracts, and why has the charity not paid you yet?"

"I hoped you could tell us more about that, since you've looked into their books."

"I haven't, but I'll ask Pio and Domenico. Maybe that's why things are moving so slowly." Maria sighed and put her hands on her head. "Oh dear, I just hope that *we* won't get into trouble now."

"What do you mean?" Lesley asked.

"Our charity is spot on and well organized. I've worked for Pio for the last two years, and I'm always paid regularly. But if your organization is in a financial mess and we're—"

The nurse had opened the door to the waiting room and called out Hope's name. I went in with her. Lesley was running late. She had to get to the train station but wanted to quickly update Maria about her own situation first.

The nurse was kind and exuberant and kept asking Hope questions in a heavily accented Italian that I hardly understood. I asked her to slow down so that I could translate the bits that I managed to extrapolate from her high-speed Neapolitan.

The nurse shook her finger at Hope and me, and laughed. "You foreigners never understand me."

I thought it better not to mention that a lot of Italians would probably struggle too. The nurse handed me a questionnaire to fill in for Hope and asked whether she thought she could be pregnant. We told her about the pregnancy test that had been negative in early October.

"October? We better check again. It's January now, and you are a young and beautiful woman."

The nurse turned to me. "How old is she exactly?"

"She turns twenty-one next month."

"You'll have to come back for a checkup with the gynecologist. She's not here today. But we can do an ultrasound to find out more."

Hope had never been to a gynecologist before. She hopped up on the bed, and I explained the procedure as best I could. The nurse switched on the screen, put some gel on Hope's naked tummy and moved the transducer slowly over it.

She saw it right away. *"Eccolo!* Here it is."

Hope understood what the nurse had seen, before I could even start to think of a gentle way to translate the news. "I don't want it."

"It's probably close to two months." The nurse looked from Hope to me, and back.

"I don't want it."

"Hope, you can take a couple of days to think about it," I said.

"Mum, there is nothing I have to think about."

The nurse nodded and pulled out a calendar. She too no longer needed any translations. "I'll get you the first available appointment with the gynecologist. What about the day after tomorrow at nine thirty?"

The nurse selected a few leaflets and asked me to make sure Hope understood the information in them, especially the possible risks of any medical procedures. I put the leaflets in my bag and recalled how Izogie had mentioned after Christmas that she wanted to go on the pill. I should have thought of it. Sex workers or not, religious or not, married or not—information about contraception and sexual health was one of the things young refugee women needed more than anything else.

***

"Do you know who the father is?" I asked in the car.

"Yes, mum."

"Your boyfriend in Pisa?"

"Mum, he is not my boyfriend."

"Will you talk to him about it?"

"Yes."

"Couldn't you stay with him?"

"Mum, you can't just go and live with somebody in Nigeria."

"You can in Italy. I have two children with a man I'm not married to. It's a Catholic country, but nobody minds."

"You can. We Nigerians can't."

The traditional values the girls kept defending always surprised me. They stood in stark opposition to their blasé behavior. Hope, Joyce and Izogie complained about everything from morning to evening but were shocked each time I vented my exasperation with the never-ending discussions with a swear word. The Tuscan population's free and imaginative use of bad language was—quite apart from great wine and beautiful beaches—one of the reasons I loved this region. Profanities and blasphemous expressions were exchanged at the village bar with the first espresso of the day. And they were—to me—the refreshing and continuous reminder that the famous rolling hills and quaint little hilltop towns could never be turned into a Disneyland as long as there was one last descendant of Dante left standing to open the day with a *"Maremma maiala!"* But it wasn't without irony that I—the Swiss woman who felt liberated by this rowdy Tuscan custom—was being reprimanded by a handful of Nigerian girls each time I hoped to benefit from the cathartic healing properties of the use of bad language. *Mamma mia*, the world was full of surprising twists and turns.

We were nearly back in Dogana when Lesley called from the train. She had left the clinic before us to travel south to visit her kids.

"What are you going to do?" she asked.

"About the job?"

"Yes."

"I don't know. It seems like a joke to stick it out like this for yet another month."

"Are you going to leave?"

"Hope is pregnant. Not a good moment to drop everything."

I added the curses *Porco cane! Porca miseria!*...but only in my thoughts. I left it to Sergio to fill in the blanks out loud once I was back home.

14

After several examinations and two more consultations, Hope got the appointment for the abortion on the last Friday of January. I picked her up in Dogana at six in the morning. It was cold and dark, and I had not been keen to get up that early.

"Mum, are you okay?" Hope was already wide awake. She still had a hard time sleeping at night.

"I'm not much of a morning person." I turned on the stereo and left it at Italian singer Lorenzo Jovanotti to make up for the lack of conversation. His *Safari* CD was still in the player from my last trip with the girls, when we had used it for a couple of improvised Italian lessons. After months of cruising through the Tuscan hinterland to the soundtrack of Nigerian hip hop and Afropop, I had started to introduce the girls to Italian music as a way to speed up their language skills.

Hope chanted along to the earworm refrain of "Fango," the first song on the CD, which also featured Ben Harper. *"Io lo so che non sono solo anche quando sono solo."* We had translated the phrase with Izogie, Joyce and Rita, and "I know that I'm not alone even when I'm alone" turned out to be the perfect line to get us through that grim January morning. Hope pressed repeat, and Jovanotti's reassuring lyrics—or Lorenzo's, as she preferred to call him—kept us company all the way to the hospital.

We arrived at the outpatient surgery a bit before seven and joined the lineup of people already waiting. After half an hour, a nurse arrived and told Hope and me to come along to a different ward. We followed her and sat down next to an elderly couple in a bright and newly restored waiting room. I pulled out my Kindle and Hope opened up *Americanah*. I had been given Chimamanda Ngozi Adichie's best seller three times in the six months since taking the job at the refugee home; twice it arrived as a parcel from Switzerland, each time sent by a friend after hearing that I was working with a group of young Nigerian women. I had enjoyed *Americanah* immensely and talked to the girls about it. Hope had not heard about the book but recommended *Half of a Yellow Sun*, the same author's gripping and heartrending book about the Biafran War. Hope also mentioned Adichie's widely known TED Talk on feminism. I had seen it but wasn't aware that Beyoncé had incorporated an excerpt into one of her recent songs.

Adichie's novels led to the books of Sefi Atta, Adaobi Tricia Nwaubani, Noo Saro-Wiwa and other contemporary Nigerian writers—many of them dealing with stories of emigration, albeit often from the point of view of, in comparison to the girls I was working with, a more privileged and educated class of people. The many troubles of Nigeria were an ever-present topic in these books, but so was the hard work, endless good spirits and immense creativity of the inhabitants of Africa's most populous country. My new reading list reminded me of the things literature accomplishes so much better than any other media. These novels managed to tell stories of a country and its people that were multifaceted and included—unlike newspaper clippings and TV news—both good and bad in their depiction of contemporary Nigeria. My understanding of this puzzling nation and its more than 180 million inhabitants was still rudimentary and conceived through the lens of the mostly

Igbo and Yoruba writers of the country's south, but at least my brain no longer lit up with the one-dimensional "sex, crime and Boko Haram" or "corruption, chaos and witchcraft" slogans when it came across the term "Nigeria." I kept being confused by the multitude of ethnicities, religions and languages that coexisted in a single country. And I was impressed but no longer surprised to discover Nigerians to be the best-educated population in the USA, boasting—according to the 2006 U.S. census—more doctorates, bachelor's and master's degrees than any other ethnic group, thus leaving white Americans far behind and eclipsing even the oft-cited stream of brainpower from Asia.

Once I started looking, the abundance of Nigerian talent started to show in Italy too. Taiye Selasi had finished *Ghana Must Go*, her brilliant debut novel, while living in Rome, and the fifty-sixth *Biennale di Venezia* was curated by Okwui Enwezor, the Nigerian curator, art critic and poet, who had also been the artistic director of the 2002 *documenta* exhibition of modern art in Kassel. In a 2014 portrait in the *Wall Street Journal*, entitled "How Okwui Enwezor Changed the Art World," the Nigerian luminary is quoted as saying: "Life is too boring if all the great stories are about Europeans and Caucasians. It's completely stupid. The world is bigger!" As a Caucasian woman, who had grown up on a steady diet of the great German, English and Russian classics, written mostly by men, I could only agree.

***

Hope was called in just after nine o'clock. She changed into a hospital gown, and I stayed with her until a nurse asked me to leave. I hugged Hope, who seemed less nervous than I was, and told her to get in touch as soon as she woke up.

I tried to call Sergio from the car. He was at work and only picked up the second time I called. I gave him an update and could hear one of his builder buddies laugh in the background. They were listening to Sergio's portable radio. I followed their example and turned on the stereo in the car. Thankful for the distraction, I started to assemble a new Italian lesson playlist from some of the songs played on Radio Deejay's most popular program. A collaboration between rapper Fedez and singer Noemi was what I'd start with. The two young, hip and talented Italian musicians were closer in age to the girls. Hope had enjoyed Jovanotti, but Izogie, Joyce and Rita hadn't been impressed. Jovanotti was in good company, though. Every time I mentioned Fela Kuti, the Nigerian creator of Afrobeat, political activist and African icon, the girls merely nodded their heads in acknowledgment and stifled a yawn. With all due respect for the "Black President," Fela's lengthy compositions were not the songs they illegally downloaded onto their smartphones.

I was halfway home and lost in these cultural and generational musings when my phone rang.

"Hello?" There was scanty reception on the countryside road leading back to my village. "Hello, who is this?" The line broke.

The phone rang again. I still couldn't hear well, but suddenly knew who I was talking to. I pulled over and jumped out of the car.

"Fola? Fola, is that you?"

Gone again. I jogged along a narrow path leading into a steep vineyard in the hope of better reception farther up. Out of breath, I did the math before calling the last incoming number once I was on top of the hill. We had not heard from Fola for more than four months.

"*Pronto?*" a female voice answered in perfect Italian.

"Hi, who's that?"

"I'm Marta. Who are you?"

"I've been called by this number."

"I haven't called anybody."

"Five minutes ago. I received two calls from this number."

"Ah, you must be the person the African girl was trying to call."

"Where is she?"

"The African girl? I don't know. We were on the same train. She asked me whether she could place a call from my phone."

"Are you still on the train?"

"No, we both just got off at Porta Susa."

"Where is Porta Susa?"

"Porta Susa is a train station in Turin." The woman was starting to get impatient. Understandably. I wanted to ask her to call me if, for some unlikely reason, she ran into Fola again. She hung up before I could.

If it had been Fola. I fiddled with my phone and wasn't sure what to do but decided I couldn't bivouac on top of a Tuscan hill in the hope of another call from Fola. I walked back down into the valley, through the long rows of immaculately pruned vines. They made the undulating slopes look like a military cemetery in the middle of winter. I got back to the car and found the key still in the ignition and the radio still on. There was Ben Harper again, this time singing "Boa Sorte" with Vanessa da Mata. Good luck, indeed. I turned on the engine and drove home.

The next call arrived half an hour later. I had just opened our front door and leaped for the phone. Another unknown number.

"Hello?"

"Mum!"

"Fola, where are you?"

"Mum, I need help. I want to come back."

"Okay, but where are you?"

"Mum, I don't know. Wait, let me pass the phone."

Before I could say anything, a pleasant male voice started to talk to me in Italian. He had an accent I had heard before but couldn't place. Fola was still at the Porta Susa train station in Turin. I turned on my computer and googled the train connections from Turin while talking to the friendly stranger, who was happy to help.

"She has to get from Porta Susa to the Porta Nuova station. Could you help her? Fola can't read."

"Yes, I'll show her."

"Thanks so much. There is a train leaving for Tuscany in a little over an hour from Porta Nuova. Is she in time to make it?"

"For sure. It doesn't take long to get there."

He handed the phone back to Fola. "Mum, I only have twenty euros."

"Get a ticket to Genoa, or another station along the south-bound line directed to Rome, and then just stay on the train. And try to call again from the train, so I know what's going on."

I didn't hear from her for the rest of the day. I called the last number on my phone and found myself talking to the friendly man again. It turned out he was from Senegal but had been living in Italy for half his life. He had helped Fola get the ticket and accompanied her to the train for the Porta Nuova station. And no, he had not seen her since.

I sat, biding my time, until I realized that I better find out what would happen if she made it back. Refugees weren't allowed to stay away from the home for more than five days unless they had a special permit. I called the vice-prefect, the government's go-to person for legal questions and problems arising in the twelve refugee homes in our Tuscan province. He told me he was going to look into it, but since Fola had run off, she didn't stand much of a chance of being allowed back into the project. I promised to keep him up to date and was relieved that he would take care of the paper work. He had always been very helpful and professional—qualities that made dealing with the crazy Italian bureaucracy much more bearable.

Late in the afternoon, I still hadn't heard back from Fola. It seemed clear at this point that she hadn't made it on the train. I searched for the number of an old friend of mine who lived in Turin. Maybe she could help in case Fola was still in town. She picked up immediately but was on holiday in Sicily. She gave me the name of a women's shelter in Turin. They didn't have any free beds and needed a referral to accept anybody into the project. The operator suggested Fola contact the police. I imagined Fola would ask anybody for help, except the police.

***

Sergio and I drove to the hospital in the early evening to pick up Hope. She looked relatively well and started a stream of phone conversations as soon as she was in the car. I looked over at Sergio, who raised his eyebrows. Manners, manners. However, it was good to know that Hope seemed to have a bunch of people in Italy who cared about her well-being. If they talked about her well-being. Her pidgin was so quick that I couldn't understand a word. She interrupted one of the phone calls to hand me a leaflet that listed excessive bleeding and several other symptoms as the warning signs to look out for during the coming days.

"Fola called."

"Fola?" Hope laughed. "Why? Where is she?"

"Somewhere in northern Italy. She is trying to come back."

"That girl, she's crazy!"

"Have you spoken to her since she left?"

"No, mum, I told you, she is not right in the head." Hope pulled *Americanah* out of her bag and told me that she had finished it. "Did you like it?"

"It's a fine book. But I was disappointed by the end."

"You didn't like the end?" I had been overjoyed that Adichie had chosen a happy ending for the book. After years of trials and tribulations, Ifemelu and Obinze, the long-lost lovers, had at last found their way back together.

"Obinze shouldn't have left his wife."

"He doesn't love her. He's still in love with Ifemelu."

"He left his family. They have a child. It's not right."

"I think that's better than being dishonest. And he's a good guy. He'll still keep taking care of his daughter and ex-wife."

"It isn't right, mum. They were married in front of God."

The Victorian moral code again. Sergio saw me shaking my head and asked what we were talking about. I signaled, "I'll tell you later" and left it at that. I wasn't in the mood to discuss the different ethical models we subscribed to. After all, Hope had just had an abortion.

***

Fola called again late on Saturday morning.

"Monte—what?" I couldn't understand where she was. She asked me to hold on, and a second later, an Italian woman told me that they were at the train station in Monterosso.

"Monterosso? On the coast?"

"Yes, in Cinque Terre. They kicked her off the train. She didn't have a valid ticket."

I checked the timetable. She could get on a southbound train in half an hour. "Could you help her get on the next train? And could you get her a ticket. I will send you the money by post, if you give me your address."

"I'm happy to help her on the train. But no, sorry, I can't give her the money for the ticket."

"She's staying with us in a refugee home. I'll make sure you get it back."

"No, I'm sorry, I can't."

I talked to Fola again and told her to get on the train the woman indicated. She would just have to keep trying getting on and off trains until we found somebody who was willing to lend her the money.

"She's in Cinque Terre?" Sergio asked, looking over my shoulder at the computer screen. "Let's go and get her. We'll be back by tonight."

"I thought about it, but no! She left on her own. She needs to get back here on her own. I'll pick her up in the city. They won't let her on the bus if she doesn't have a ticket, but that's it."

"You're sure?"

"I'm sure! I'm happy if she comes back, but the rules will have to change."

"Fine. You're the boss. When will she arrive?"

"I don't know. It depends on how often they kick her off the train. She doesn't—*mamma mia*, I'm such an idiot!" I couldn't believe I hadn't thought of it earlier.

"What?" Sergio looked at me.

"She doesn't *need* the money for the ticket!"

I had been so worried and agitated since Fola first called that I had totally forgotten that I could buy a ticket online in her name. She didn't need a printout. A note with the ticket code and the exact car and seat number would be enough, as long as she traveled on an express train and not on one of the much more old-fashioned regional trains. I checked the connections. This was making things a lot easier.

Now the only question was how Fola would jot down the details of her ticket. She could spell the letters of her name, but I didn't think she knew how to write the whole alphabet or any numbers. And the ticket code was a confusing mix of both. She would have to find somebody with pen and paper who could write everything down for her. I looked through the numbers of incoming calls on my phone and dialed the last one. Luckily, she was still with the Italian woman from before.

"Mum?"

"Fola, could you pass me to the lady again? She has to write something down for you."

"She's not here anymore."

"But what about the phone?"

"Mum, this is my phone. A man from Ghana gave it to me last night at the station in Genoa. He said there is only a little money on it."

"That's great! Don't worry about the credit, I can keep calling you. You spent the night in Genoa?"

"Yes, at the station."

I knew it had been snowing in Turin. I didn't even want to imagine how she had managed to get through an icy cold winter night in front of Genoa's train station. She could tell me later. I went back to the computer to check the connections.

"Fola, I'm getting your ticket now. I can pay for it online. I will send you a text message with the reservation number. You have seat number sixteen in car eight. Can you remember that? Sixteen is ten plus six."

"Eight and sixteen. I'll remember. I know the numbers!"

"Right, sorry. So just remember car eight and seat sixteen, and show my text message to the conductor on the train."

"Okay, mum."

"Oh, and Fola, the ticket is only valid for this exact train, which leaves in twenty minutes. It is directed to Rome. Can you see it on the display?"

"Rome?"

"Yes, but wait. It might say Napoli, for Naples. It depends on the final destination of the train. Can you read 'Roma' on the big sign where all the trains are listed?"

"Mum?"

"It says either 'Roma' or 'Napoli.' Roma is spelled R-O-M-A. Fola?"

"Mum?"

"Can you read the sign?"

"No."

Hell, I was pissed off. I kept reading about Nigerians piling up insane numbers of master's degrees and doctorates, and here I was trying to teach a girl who had not even been taught to spell a four-letter word that wasn't her own name. How was it possible that Nigeria's oil money hadn't been invested into a public school system that guaranteed literacy for every kid? These millions could have built schools for girls like Fola and Izogie and changed their lives. Instead, they had been syphoned out of the country and lay safely stored away in Swiss bank accounts. Few things could stall the world's literacy rates as much as a handful of dictators and corrupt politicians linked to a smug banker or two in my home country.

"Mum?"

"Forget it. Just do as you did 'til now."

"Okay, I'll ask again."

The usual approach worked again. Fola called me from the train, and I left a couple of hours later to pick her up in the city. I thought of the girls' complaints about Fola while I waited for her at the station. Hope and Izogie had not missed her, since she cleaned and helped even less in the house than everybody else. I hoped she would be more proactive now that she knew what the options were out there. Surely, her return would serve as a good reminder for the others that it was worth putting in an effort during their time at the house.

Fola got off the train looking disheveled, and different. It took me a moment to realize that she had lost a lot of weight. She was still curvy but looked like she weighed much less than when I had seen her last. She was pulling a small wheeled suitcase and wore a thin fake black leather jacket with a pair of striped leggings. I was cold just looking at her.

We walked to the car park, and I told her to wait for a moment. The lock on the Dacia's back door was broken, and I had to get inside the car to open it awkwardly with a long wooden stick from the back seat for Fola's luggage. Fixing it was the first item on the list once I got paid. When I got out of the car again, a black Alfa Romeo had stopped next to Fola. An elderly man was talking to her while rubbing his thumb, first and middle fingers together, the Italian hand gesture for money. What, I wondered, did he want to pay her for? I could feel myself turn into Superwoman, or better yet, Jessica Jones. I was just going to pull the sleazebag out of his fancy car and bang his head against the trunk. Once. And then some more.

"Sorry," he said, as soon as he realized that Fola wasn't alone. "I must have mistaken her for somebody else. I know a girl who looks just like her."

"I'm sure you do!"

My superpower seemed to show. He was off and out of the parking lot before I could even start to tell him what I thought of him. I watched the Alfa Romeo disappear around the corner and was annoyed that he got away with it. Just as Johns do. *Ma vaffanculo!* I should have pulled him by his ear to his wife, who was surely at home imagining her husband at the soccer game while she kneaded the pasta dough. No need to bang his head if his wife could hit him with the rolling pin. But maybe his wife wasn't eager for Superwoman to intervene in her domestic affairs. Maybe she was quite happy with their unspoken arrangement and preferred spending the weekend wearing an old apron to prepare her famous homemade lasagna than having to search the drawers for sexy underwear.

I got into the car and put my seatbelt on. "Sorry, what a prick!"

Fola just waved her hand and didn't seem bothered, whereas I felt I had to excuse the actions of an elderly Italian man. As if his crappy behavior was my responsibility. Maybe it was white guilt. I had gotten used to being ripped off from time to time by Italian gas station clerks and fruit dealers selling oranges out of the back of a truck. I had learned the hard and rather expensive way that *prezzo d'amici* didn't really mean "friendship price" but exactly the opposite—at least if enthusiastically offered by an Italian to a client who spoke with a thick Swiss accent. I had gotten used to being an easy target for the "foreigner-only price list," but in my nearly two decades in Italy, I never had to ward off sex buyers in search of a prostitute just because of the color of my skin.

"How are you?" I asked Fola.

"Mum, thank you. Better. It's good to be back."

"What happened? Where have you been?"

"It's a long story."

"I can imagine. And I'd like to hear it."

"Mum, can I make a phone call—"

"Fola, I just spent two days trying to help you get back here. Could you *please* let me know what exactly has been going on?"

"Okay, mum."

"Where have you been?"

Fola cleared her voice and started to tell me what had happened in the months after she disappeared. "I had met this man from Senegal. One of the door-to-door vendors who sometimes came to Dogana. I talked to him. He was nice. He invited me to come for a ride with him to Turin. I said yes, because I didn't know it was so far away."

"Why didn't you call?"

"He took my phone. He took me to his flat and told me I wasn't allowed to go out. He said he wanted to marry me. But he was jealous. He locked me in his apartment in Turin."

"And then?"

"He threatened me and didn't let me out. I had to cook and wait for him at home. He said he would marry me. He bought me clothes, but I didn't want to get married to him. Two days ago, he forgot to lock the door when he went out, and I took my chance and left."

"Fola, I haven't heard from you for nearly five months... are you seriously telling me that you've been locked up in this man's house for all that time?"

"Yes, mum."

"And once you saw that the door wasn't locked, you didn't just run out but packed your suitcase first?'

"Mum, I knew he wouldn't be back for the whole day. He went to work. And I didn't know what would happen. I wanted to be sure I had some warm clothes."

I kept asking questions, and Fola repeated what she had already told me. It seemed an unlikely story, and wasn't what I had expected to hear, but she insisted that she had just been unlucky in meeting the wrong man.

"Look, I'll try to help you, but it isn't decided yet whether you'll be allowed to stay at the house again. However, we'll try to figure something out."

"Thank you, mum." Fola leaned back, closed her eyes and fell asleep.

15

Fola had been back at the refuge for three days when another phone call arrived. I was having my early-morning cappuccino at our table in the olive grove. It was chilly, but the ten minutes every morning in the winter sun in the middle of fifty perfectly poised trees, with that view, a cat sleeping on the table and a dog running its laps, managed to keep me sane. At least for the first ten minutes of the day. I checked the vibrating phone on the table. Another unknown number. I had an odd presentiment, which was confirmed as soon as I heard Precious's unmistakable smoky voice. Maybe I was starting to pick up some of Cassandra's clairvoyant abilities after all.

"Mum?"

"Precious?"

"I want to come back. Help me, mum, *please!*"

She sounded dreadful. Frightened. And her voice was void of the arrogant and self-important attitude that used to irritate me at least once a day. Nevertheless, I thought the timing was strange. Two girls disappeared—one in September and one in October—and reappeared, just like that, one after the other, three days apart?

"Did you talk to Fola?"

"No! But mum, can you call me on this number? This isn't my phone."

I called her back and explained that Fola had just returned.

"Why are you calling me now after not getting in touch for months?"

"You told us to call you if we ever needed help. I need help, mum. Now."

"Where are you?"

"I'm in Rome. I'll pass you to the person I'm staying with."

"Hello?" A man started talking to me in Italian with a strong accent. He had a friendly voice and was eager to explain.

"Precious is staying with me and my wife. I got off the train yesterday and saw her standing on the platform. She looked lost. And scared. I thought something bad must have happened to this girl. I asked her whether she needed help. It's snowing in Turin, but she didn't even have a jacket."

"In Turin? She just told me she's in Rome!"

"No, no, we're in Turin. I met her at the Porta Nuova station."

Turin? Again? Precious knew how to read and write, why had she thought she was in Rome? I didn't know what to make of it, but the man on the phone had a nice and gentle voice and seemed truly concerned about her.

"Do you know what happened to her?"

"No, she didn't talk. She was scared when I approached her, but in the end decided to come with me. She said she had run away. She got on a train in Milan and got off at the first station. My wife got clean clothes at the Caritas charity nearby. Hers were all dirty. But she needs a place to stay. She can't stay with us."

"What did she tell you?"

"She said she had been locked up somewhere and managed to run away. But she isn't saying anything else. She said this morning that she stayed at a shelter in Tuscany. She showed me a slip of paper with your number on it."

"Can you help her to get back to the train station?" I asked. "I can get the ticket for her now, but she'll have to be on the train I make the reservation for."

"I'm starting work at ten. I can accompany her to the station before that."

With a valid ticket, the trip would be easier for Precious than it was for Fola. But I didn't want to take any chances. Not everybody would be as supportive as the man on the phone.

"Do you think you could buy her a simple phone? I can send you the money for it, if you text me your address."

"Don't' worry about the money. She can have my old phone, and I'll get her a SIM card before we get to the station. I'm just relieved that she has a place to go."

"That is very kind of you, thank you. Where are you from?" I wasn't good at recognizing accents, but even I could tell that his wasn't Nigerian.

"I'm from Gambia. It's a small country, most people have never heard of it. Don't worry if you don't know it."

I knew the Gambia. But only because I had looked up the country's location a few days before, after chatting with a group of young Gambians who stayed at the refugee home that had recently opened in my Tuscan village. The refugee home was run by a different charity than the one I worked for in Dogana, but I kept meeting the refugees staying there when I was picking up our kids from school. Apart from a stretch of coastline on the Atlantic, the Gambia, the smallest country on Africa's mainland, is entirely surrounded by Senegal. As a citizen of a small country, I had always been curious about the characteristics of other small countries, and in the case of the Gambia, I would soon get the chance to find out more.

***

Precious made it back on the same day. She was already waiting for me when I arrived at the station and laughed when she got into the car. No trace of the shaky voice I had heard on the phone.

"Mum, now you're laughing at me."

"Not at all. It looks like you're the one laughing."

"Because I know what you think. You think, see this stupid girl, how many times have I told her not to run away?"

I had indeed thought a few things along these lines. And I also said them out loud when I called Lesley to tell her about Precious's phone call. Lesley had always maintained that Precious and Fola were likely to come back once they realized what type of life awaited them in the big cities they had been yearning for.

"How are you?"

"I'm fine, mum." Precious laughed again. Seemingly an entirely different woman from the one I had talked to early this morning.

"What happened? Why did you leave?"

"Mum, I didn't come back to the house that day because an Italian man invited me to come with him for a ride. He said I'd be back in the evening. He took me to Milan. When I realized how far it was, I decided to come back a couple of days later. But when I wanted to leave, he didn't let me. He locked me in his flat. I didn't have a key. I couldn't go outside."

"And let me see, you decided to run off the other day because he forgot to lock the door?"

"Yes, that's exactly what happened!"

"Precious—"

"Mum, you don't believe me?"

"Not really, no."

"*Mum!* I'm telling the truth!"

"And your truth sounds exactly like the one Fola told me three days ago. Just that in her case the man who locked her up wasn't from Italy but from Senegal."

"Was Fola locked up too?"

"Yes, in Turin."

"I wasn't in Turin, mum. I was in Milan. I ran off and just got on the first train I could find. I wanted to get as far away as possible."

"..."

"Mum, it's true. Ask the man who called you. He found me at the station. I had just arrived and didn't know where to go!"

"Right."

"Mum, are you saying I'm lying?"

"I don't have a clue, but you're definitely not telling me everything. Remember when you didn't come back that day from the city? You'd told Hope and Joyce that you had already called me to let me know that you weren't coming back on the early bus in time for yoga. But you hadn't."

"That's not true, mum. I never told them that."

"So why would they have said so when they got back?"

"I don't know why they told you this. I don't know what's going on inside their heads. I can only speak for myself."

"Look, let's not argue. We don't even know yet whether you'll be allowed to stay at the house again. But if so, we'll have to find a way to work things out differently. You have to start telling us what's going on. Like, what's *really* going on."

"I told you! This Italian guy took me to Milan. He locked me in the flat. I wasn't allowed to go outside."

"Precious, two girls disappear for months and then come back telling me exactly the same story? You don't think that's a little strange?"

151

"Mum, there are lots of crazy men in the world."

That for sure was true.

"Is it my fault if the same thing happened to Fola? I can only tell you what I know. I ran off as soon as I could. And I called you. Remember, you told us to hold on to your number? In case we ever needed help. You promised you would help."

And that was true too. It was just that I had envisioned this business of helping to be a much more straightforward affair.

I drove Precious back to the house and told her that she would sleep in the room with Hope and Joyce from now on. She had shared with Izogie before, but Rita had taken up her old bed in the meantime. And Izogie didn't want to share with her again, since Precious had borrowed twenty euros from her without ever paying it back.

"What happened to your smartphone? The one you bought in autumn. Remember, you still owe Izogie money for it?"

"Mum, this guy, he took it away. I didn't have a phone. I couldn't call anybody."

***

Precious received a loud and overexcited welcome from everybody, and I was relieved to see that the old squabbles were no longer an issue. Or at least not for the moment.

Lesley was frying plantains in the kitchen and asked whether I wanted to stay for dinner. I declined, as I had already called Sergio to tell him that I'd be back in time to prepare dinner. Hope's abortion and the improvised rescue missions for Fola and Precious had taken their toll on the balance of our family life, and I wanted to give Sergio a break from all the cooking. Lesley wrapped some plantains in paper towels for me to take home, and Fola handed me a piece of paper she wanted me to read through before I left. It was a letter from the police in Turin, which requested she present herself at the immigration office where she had lodged her original asylum request. I read the letter aloud for Lesley to hear. The police had stopped Fola on a provincial road not far from Turin a couple of days before she made her way back to Dogana.

"So this is why you came back?" Lesley asked Fola, turning around from the stove.

"No, mum, I told you both. I ran away. The police stopped me after that. I was on a bus, and the foreigners who didn't have documents were taken to the station."

"Where was the bus going?"

"Mum, I don't know. I just ran out of the house and took the first bus I saw passing by."

I listened to Lesley and Fola's conversation and started googling. The letter from the police didn't state why Fola had been stopped. It indicated, however, the exact road where she had been picked up. The address turned out to be an access road to the Turin-Milan highway. I googled the location again, this time with the term "prostitution," and found several newspaper articles reporting the surge of daytime streetwalking in that exact area. I told Fola and Lesley about my findings. Lesley rolled her eyes. Fola insisted that it wasn't her fault that the bus had been stopped exactly in that area and handed me another letter—this one from a lawyer in Turin, who informed her in legalese about the state of her asylum request at the immigration office in Turin.

"You lodged an asylum request in Turin? Why? You already did that here."

"Mum, the man who locked me up took me to the lawyer. He wanted to marry me and said I needed documents."

I called the phone number on the letterhead, hoping to get some clues to what had happened and who this man was from the lawyer who had lodged the request for her. The secretary put me through, and the lawyer confirmed that Fola had indeed started the process for an asylum request in Turin, but she couldn't remember who had accompanied Fola to her office.

"Did you know that Fola already lodged a request here?"

"I didn't." From her voice I imagined that I was speaking with a chain-smoking fiftysomething woman with short gray hair and understanding eyes. "I wouldn't have started the process otherwise. You can't lodge a request in two different places. They would have interrupted the procedure in Turin once they would have found out after taking her fingerprints."

"Why didn't they already take them?"

"The immigration office in Turin is flooded to such an extent that it can take literally forever to get an appointment. Fola has been on the waiting list for two months, but they haven't called yet to give us the appointment. Please send a fax to the immigration office to let them know that she doesn't need it anymore."

"Is it really necessary to send a fax?" I hadn't sent a fax in a decade or so, and I didn't look forward to standing in line at our local post office to take up the custom again.

"They are desperately understaffed at the immigration office, but they are trying very hard to make the best of the situation. So, yes, please let them know that she doesn't need the slot on the waiting list any longer before they start losing time by digging out her request for nothing."

Lesley and I asked Fola some more questions. The same story again. She would never prostitute herself; she had just been unlucky in falling for the wrong guy.

I drove home late again, and was so tired and frustrated that I ate up all the fried plantains Lesley had prepared for me right in the car. Precious had truly sounded desperate in the morning, but from the moment she got into my car, she just seemed to be telling me a heap of bullshit. And Fola's story was so full of holes that I didn't even know anymore what to say to her. It was maddening. The more I found out, the less I knew, and the longer I knew the girls, the less I understood. We seemed to live in parallel universes, and no matter how much time we spent together, nothing could fuse, or even just link, our completely different worlds.

***

Sergio was home when I arrived and had already picked up the kids at his parents'.

"Sorry it took longer than I thought. Hungry?"

"Yes! Why so late again?"

I gave Sergio a quick update on the latest events.

He opened a bottle of Montecucco wine and sighed a couple of times. "You probably don't want to hear this, but I really can't quite see the point of what you're doing."

"I know. Me neither. At least not at the moment." I grabbed my glass, tempted to just down it. "We need to figure out a better approach as soon as the new organization moves in."

"Have you heard from them?"

"No, not yet. I guess they are still working their way through the financial mess Teresa must have left behind."

"No surprises there! Have a shower, I'll figure out something for dinner."

"*Grazie!*"

I hugged the kids, who, mesmerized by the TV, were totally

oblivious to not having eaten yet.

The doorbell rang when I was already under the shower. I heard Sergio open the window and shout something. He stormed into the bathroom a couple of minutes later.

"So who is this now?"

"Who is who?"

"The young man outside."

"Who's outside?" I didn't have a clue what he was talking about.

"There's a young African men standing in front of our gate, and he's asking for my sister."

"For your sister? You don't have a sister."

"Exactly! Which is why I would like to know why he seems to think that I'm your brother?" There was a lot of steam in our small bathroom, and some of it seemed to come right out of Sergio's nostrils. "He says you told him to come by."

"Now I know! Shit, I totally forgot." I wrapped my wet hair into a towel and looked out of the window. "Aziz, right?"

"Hello, yes, it's Aziz. I'm very sorry to disturb you sister, but you told me last week that you might have some warm jackets for us."

"Yes, for sure. Sorry, I had a crazy week and didn't get to it yet. Just give me a moment." I turned to Sergio and explained that I had met Aziz and three of his friends on the way home a few days ago. They were walking along the country road that leads to our house, and I stopped to ask whether they needed any clothes, since two of them weren't wearing jackets in the freezing weather. "They are staying in the refugee home in the village. They have only just arrived, and they obviously don't have enough warm clothes yet."

Sergio threw his arms into the air. "Great! So Dogana wasn't enough? Now, you also help out at the refugee home in our town? Brava! Let me ask around. I'm sure we can find some more work for you!"

"C'mon! I just happen to know that it can be tricky to find a lot of clothes in the right size quickly. And since it's cold—"

Sergio was no longer listening and had pulled out the ladder to get up under the roof to rummage through our small storage space in the attic. He bumped his head a couple of times and, several curses later, came down with three of his soccer club winter jackets that I had been wanting to give to the Red Cross for ages.

"Where are the other ones?" he asked.

"Which ones?" I had actually already thrown out a few a couple of years ago.

He fired out a few more profanities, put the jackets into a plastic bag and went downstairs to give them to Aziz. I told the kids to turn off the TV and put the pasta water on.

"Nice guy that Aziz," Sergio said, as he was coming back inside. "What do you think?"

"I told you, I only met him very briefly, but yes, he seemed really nice."

"Nice, young and also rather good-looking." Sergio stood, arms crossed, in the middle of the kitchen and looked at me, waiting for a reaction.

I waved him out of the way and rummaged in the fridge for a jar of my mother-in-law's Tuscan ragù. I had better make sure my newfound Italian "brother" got something to eat. And quickly.

After a plate of pasta, Sergio seemed less cantankerous and I tried to explain the misunderstanding.

"You know, Lesley often calls me 'sister.' I think it's just a friendly way in West Africa to address or refer to people you like."

"I'm fine with that," Sergio said while filling the children's and his own plate with a second serving of penne al ragù, "as long as it's Lesley."

***

Fola and I were early for her appointment at the immigration office on Friday morning. Fola was for once no longer her exuberant and confident self but sat quietly next to me on a plastic chair, biting her fingernails. I hoped we'd end up talking to the young, friendly policewoman, but the short bald-headed immigration officer arrived instead. He didn't even ask us into his office and made it clear right in the waiting room that he had not the least intention of wasting any of his precious time on stuff like this.

"You know what she has been doing in Turin?" The officer directed his words to me without acknowledging Fola, who was standing right beside me.

"I'm not exactly sure, but—"

"She has been stopped for prostitution. I'll make a note to confirm that she presented herself here as ordered by the police in Turin. But I can't see why she has to be allowed into the project again. She had her chance."

"We all deserve a second chance."

"We all make our decisions and have to live with them."

"Fair enough. At least for us." I hated this guy. "I'm not sure, though, how informed my decision-making process would be if I was being threatened and told by society that working as a prostitute was the only spot in the food chain available to me."

"Say what you want, she won't get her permit of stay from me.

She should have stayed here and picked it up when it was ready last autumn." He turned around and went back into his office without any further ado.

"Mum?" Fola didn't need a translation to understand that things weren't looking good.

"I'm going to talk to the vice-prefect. He promised to help." I called the prefecture and was put on hold for a while but got through to the vice-prefect in the end.

"Sorry, things are crazy here with all the arrivals. And to think that it isn't even spring yet. If the numbers keep rising like this, the situation in 2015 will be worse than anything we've seen so far."

The vice-prefect's assessment of the situation in the Mediterranean would be proven right a few months later. It was just that, unforeseen by the press, humanitarian organizations and immigration experts alike, the vast majority of Syrian refugees arriving on Europe's shores would not enter the continent via the long-trodden route from Libya to Italy's south but by embarking from Turkey for a handful of tiny Greek islands in the Aegean Sea.

I told the vice-prefect about our depressing encounter with the immigration officer, hoping for some better news from his side. I couldn't resist mentioning that I thought it extremely unprofessional of the officer to discuss the issue at hand standing up in the waiting area with lots of other people listening.

"Let me ask you something," the vice-prefect interrupted my little speech. "Do you have an Italian passport?"

I had no idea what my passport had to do with Fola's permit of stay. "No, I don't. Why?"

"Good. And make sure you *never*, *ever* apply for one. We're a country of hopeless nitwits! Just hold on to your Swiss citizenship. I wish I could say the same for me!"

I had to laugh. If anybody deserved a Swiss passport, it was the vice-prefect. He hailed from southern Italy, but his meticulous and thorough work ethic made him seem much more like a born and bred Swiss citizen than me. "I won't ever apply for one, I promise. But what about this immigration officer of yours?"

"He's a nightmare. And a show-off. He knows the prefecture has the final say, but he just loves to make everybody's life as difficult as possible. I'm used to it by now. We'll find a way."

"Thanks a lot."

"Just one more thing. You are absolutely positive you want the two girls back at your house?"

"Yes. What else am I supposed to do?"

"You know they only came back because they hadn't managed to find anything better?" This was exactly what Lesley had said when she heard that Precious was on her way back.

"I can't blame them."

"Okay, I'll be in touch. I can't promise, but I hope you'll be able to pick up the documents next week."

"I'll be skiing in Switzerland next week."

"Skiing in the Swiss Alps? I wouldn't come back at all, then, if I was you!"

I put my phone away.

Fola was looking at her fingernails, which she had bitten to the quick. "What is going to happen, mum? You think I can't stay?"

"The vice-prefect is trying to sort this out, but he can't guarantee it will work out."

"Mum..."

"What?"

"I can't go back. Please!"

160

"Fola, what happened in Turin?"

"Turin wasn't good."

"In what sense? What wasn't good?"

Moisture started to collect in Fola's big brown eyes, until two tears swelled over. I watched the two shiny drops hang on to Fola's eyelashes for a second or two before they slowly made their way down her cheeks. I had worked with the girls for half a year and had seen them angry, happy, bored, depressed, excited and angry again—but none of them had ever cried. Not once.

"Fola, remember, there is another option if you can't stay with us." The vice-prefect had already put me in touch with a charity in Pisa that worked with victims of human trafficking, especially with women who had been exploited and forced into prostitution. "They can help you. But you have to tell them what's going on."

"Mum, nothing is going on. I don't want to go to another place. I just want to stay with the other girls." The two tears had left a salty trail on Fola's cheeks. No new ones had formed. The door had already been shut again.

I had called the operator of the women's shelter in Pisa the day before. She was friendly and very frank. She had explained that they could find a spot for Fola in the project, but she had to be ready to make a fresh start. She didn't have to denounce anybody, since this was often the tricky point, which, similar to the dynamics of the Mafia, meant people didn't dare to make a change since they were too afraid of the possible consequences. But anybody entering their project had to entirely cut the ties to their old life. Whatever had happened to Fola in Turin, I knew even before asking her that she wasn't ready for this. The SIM cards or slips of papers, stored away in plastic bags or hidden in bras and underpants to protect them from getting wet during the crossing, and filled to the edges with phone numbers of family, friends and friends of friends, were the most precious thing any traveler could hold on to when making the perilous passage from one side of the Mediterranean to the other.

16

"Stay in second gear!" Lesley said.

"Mum, do as Lesley says!" Rita, Izogie and Joyce shouted simultaneously from the back.

Both my hands nervously clutched the steering wheel. I had only ever owned a bicycle in Switzerland and wasn't used to driving on snow. To make up for this, destiny had provided me with the company of four Nigerians, who of course turned out to be experts in the matter.

I had promised Lesley I'd pick her up at eight in the morning. Public transport wasn't going up to Dogana until the road was cleared, and Lesley's battered Fiat Uno only had summer tires. And Lesley had to catch the train. She was adamant about that. She could see her kids only once a week. A ridiculous snowstorm wasn't going to get in the way of the most treasured hour of her week.

Joyce, Rita and Izogie had insisted on coming along to the station. I had tried to convince them to stay at the house, but the sight of the icy white powder—their first snow—didn't intimidate them in the least. They had traveled under far worse conditions. They had fooled around a bit and thrown a couple of snowballs before they got into the car. A Nigerian friend of Rita's was celebrating her birthday in Florence, and the girls were all dressed up for their night out on the town.

"You can change gear now," Lesley said.

"Mum, change gear!" The backseat drivers' echoed.

"I can see that!"

Farther down in the valley, the layer of snow had thinned out and turned slushy, and I surely didn't need four Nigerians in elaborate weaves pointing it out to me. Unlike them, *I* had seen snow before in my life. But so had Lesley, who had learned to drive when she lived in a village in the Sila mountains in Calabria. Even though it was all the way down in southern Italy, the village got snowed in every winter. If we had to pull out the tire chains, my Igbo colleague would be the person in the car who knew how to handle the situation.

"Thanks again for picking me up," Lesley said, once we had made it to the station. "Are you okay?"

"Yes. But I still think you should have called the children's home and told them you needed to postpone your visit a day or two because of the weather."

"I can't postpone seeing my children. They expect me! Plus, my husband is just waiting for me to not show up on time. The moment he heard of it, he'd call his lawyer, and who knows what they'd manage to make of it? With the connections they have, they could easily find a famous meteorologist who'd be more than happy to attest that it hadn't been snowing in Tuscany today."

"I could testify for you! We Swiss always make a good impression."

"A Swiss who can't even mount a pair of snow chains? Forget it!"

Lesley and I were still operating in a vacuum. We had no support from the organization that had hired us, and the new charity kept pushing the take-over date further away. I was tired of this whole situation, but I was dealing with peanuts compared to what Lesley was going through.

***

A few days later, I was skidding on snow again. This time I was, however, entirely in control. I had spent all my winter holidays as a child downhill skiing in the Swiss Alps, and not many things managed to cheer me up as much as tackling a steep mountain slope on top of a fast pair of skis. To make sure the family tradition was passed on to her grandchildren, my mother invited us each year for a holiday in Braunwald, a village in the Glarus Alps two hours from Zurich. Sergio couldn't take holidays at that time of the year, a fact he cherished, as he dreaded having to spend a whole week in the snow with a group of overexcited Swiss German speakers. I still planned to show him Braunwald one day, for its beautiful view over the snow-capped mountains and the laid-back vibe in the small outmoded village, which, accessible only by cliff railway, had been spared mass touristic invasion.

But that winter, the Alpine air and company of Swiss friends and family didn't cheer me up as much as they always had during past holidays. I felt under the weather, and the backache that had plagued me all winter got worse while I was skiing. It was running into a friend of a friend towards the end of the week that made me forget my aching bones for a while. Katrin, the owner of the chalet where my friends were staying, spotted me in the lineup for the ski lift and called out and signaled for me to wait for her. The friends we had in common had already told her about my job and she wanted to hear more about it. Katrin knew Tuscany well. Her brother had emigrated to Pienza, where he ran an organic farm, and Katrin wondered how the current wave of immigration was received in the villages of the Tuscan countryside. We grabbed a T-bar lift together, and I told her a bit about the ups and downs of my job.

"That all sounds challenging," Katrin said. She pushed her ski goggles above her helmet and looked over at me. "And where exactly are the girls from?"

"Nigeria."

"You said so. But I mean where in Nigeria?" This was the first time anybody had asked me to be so precise. Nigeria may be Africa's most populous country, and its biggest economy, but most Europeans would have a hard time pinpointing its exact location on a map, let alone remember any specific part of it.

"Most of them are from Edo State, which is in the southeastern—"

"Edo State! I came through Benin City when I was traveling Nigeria."

"You traveled in Nigeria?"

"Yes. Albeit more than twenty years ago."

"Wow. Why did you choose Nigeria? I wouldn't have thought it was a popular place to visit twenty years ago."

The country was ruled by Sani Abacha for most of the nineties. The corrupt dictator and his military junta didn't exactly turn Nigeria into a sought-after holiday destination. As I knew from Lesley, Abacha had spent most of his time looting the country's infrastructure and resources, and stashing billions of dollars in numbered bank accounts in Switzerland and other countries in Europe.

"I worked as a sound technician for Femi Kuti's Switzerland tour. That's why I started my trip in Nigeria. I stayed with Femi and his sisters in Lagos for a while." My skis crossed and I had to hold on to Katrin's arm to regain my balance. I hadn't fallen off a ski lift since I was a teenager, but hearing that I shared a T-bar with a woman who had worked with the Kuti family nearly interrupted my thirty-year streak.

"Yeni and Sola were part of the band too. Sadly, Sola died in 1997, only a few months after Fela's death."

"Did you meet Fela too?"

"Of course! We'd visit him once a week. His health was already deteriorating then, but he still played at the Shrine."

"You heard Fela live at the Shrine?"

"Yep, it was great. I even ended up mixing a couple of concerts at the Shrine, when Femi played there with his own band."

I would have pinched myself, if I hadn't been wrapped up in several layers of thermal underwear and skiing gear. I had listened (and living-room danced) to Fela Kuti throughout the winter. But the father of Afrobeat isn't worshipped just for his immense musical legacy that nearly two decades after his death keeps influencing African, European and American musicians alike. Nigerians remember Fela Anikulapo Kuti as a political activist and enfant terrible, who continued to openly criticize the military junta even after his time in prison and the killing of his mother by soldiers. In one way or another, Fela was mentioned in most of the contemporary Nigerian novels that I had read. And *Looking for Transwonderland*, Noo Saro-Wiwa's travel memoir of her time in Nigeria, ends with a scene about a night out at the New Afrika Shrine concert hall, the replacement of the old Afrika Shine created by Fela in 1970, in Lagos. The passage beautifully captures all the headache, resilience, worry and inspiration the daughter of Nigerian writer and activist Ken Saro-Wiwa encountered during her exploration of the country of her ancestors.

Later that day, I sat at a long table, sticking bite-sized pieces of bread onto a long fork to swirl them through melted cheese.

After our chance encounter on the ski lift, Katrin and I had decided get everyone together for a fondue at her chalet. We pulled out gooey forks of cheese from the terra-cotta fondue set in the middle of the table, while I updated everybody on our ski-lift conversation, and Katrin filled in bits about her travel in Nigeria and the time she spent with the Kuti family in Lagos.

"Did they think you are weird?" my son asked, with the lack of political correctness only children can pull off. I was about to shush him, but Katrin answered first.

"They actually did!"

"Because you look different?"

"No, not because of that. But they thought I wasn't very sophisticated. Fela's daughters kept calling me bush girl."

Everybody stopped swirling forks and turned to look at the blonde-haired woman at the head of the table. "They called *you* bush girl?" my oldest brother said.

"Yes." Katrin laughed. "Yeni and Sola did."

"But why?" I asked.

Katrin rolled her eyes and laughed again. "I guess my manners weren't up to scratch."

"Your manners?"

I could imagine the locals of the Glarus Alps being accused of rude behavior. I still hadn't found out whether their lack of social skills was because of centuries of hard and secluded mountain life or because they decided to be grumpy with tourists on principle. But Katrin was a friendly and educated woman who had grown up in the city and now worked as a sound technician at the most prestigious theater in Switzerland.

"What did you do to make them think that?" I asked.

"It wasn't what I did. More what I *didn't* do. I was backpacking. Clothes, manicures and elegant hairdos weren't my big concerns.

168

I must have looked like a total tramp to them."

"Right, but you were traveling, after all."

"Sure, but you should see Nigerian women tackle the crazy Lagos traffic. Traveling is no excuse for bad looks."

I knew what she meant. I followed several locals from Lagos and Port Harcourt on Instagram, and their impeccable looks and great styling always made me uncomfortably aware of the fact that I was scrolling through their feeds wearing my shaggy pajama bottoms and a tattered sweater.

"So it was just about different ways of dressing?" one of my brothers asked.

"No, it was about different customs too. Some things I did felt rude to them."

"Like what?"

"Like... Wait, I'll show you. Who wants a coffee?" Several hands went up in the air, and Katrin got up and put the coffee maker on. She put milk and sugar on the table and poured the coffee into small espresso cups before sitting back down.

"So what?" I asked.

"I just put the coffee on the table for you to serve yourself. That would be considered rude in Nigeria, or at least in the parts of the country I have been to."

"Why?"

"Because it isn't a respectful way to treat your guests. If you offer somebody tea, you'll ask them how much sugar and how much milk they'd like and prepare it before handing them the cup. Sola and Yeni couldn't believe I didn't know that. Or that I didn't properly accompany my guests when they left. I'd take them to the door, but the sisters reminded me that the least I could do was accompany them all the way to the door of their car." Katrin looked around the table and laughed. "Only a bush

169

girl like me didn't know that this was the minimum you could expect when visiting somebody."

We scratched our heads and discussed different local customs until the end of our dinner. I observed to Martin, the friend sitting next to me, that it was rather amusing that I had tried to get away from anything Nigerian for a week and the country had managed to catch up with me even in a little-known and out-of-the-way mountain valley.

"This valley isn't quite as backwards as you think," Martin said.

"I didn't mean any offense. I just wouldn't have expected to run into somebody who has met Fela Kuti in person on a ski lift in Braunwald."

"Hold on. You have to see this video!" Martin got up to get his iPad. He had grown up in Glarus and was the reason that we holidayed in this part of the Swiss Alps. Martin had escaped the narrow mountain valley as a young man, but I always envied him a bit. The Alps were such a miracle of nature and—at least to me—much more fascinating then the hills of the village close to the German border where I had grown up.

"You could have run into people here who have traveled Nigeria already long before any of us were born," Martin said, back at the table with his tablet.

"Any of us?" I pointed to my mum. She was seventy-five, after all.

"Yep, way before your mum was born."

He went on Facebook and turned up the volume so that the whole table could listen to an affable owner of a textile factory near Glarus recount the story of Conrad Blumer, one of the founders of the factory. I already knew about the textile industry in the canton of Glarus. Down in the valley, the beautiful Hänggitürme, the towers where the dyed lengths of material

170

were hung up to dry, still testified to it. The vibrant fabrics dangling from tall buildings in the middle of the Swiss Alps must have been a striking sight. Blumer had brought the patterns back from his travels in India and Indonesia in 1823. He had copied them into his notebook and his factory had started to hand-print them on material intended for sale in India, Indonesia, Senegal and Nigeria. The locals appreciated the paisley pattern Blumer had brought back from India, and soon the cloth printed with it was a success in Switzerland too.

My daughter looked down at the Glarner Tüechli, the red handkerchief she was wearing around her neck. It was the famous printed cloth the engaging local on Martin's iPad was talking about. My mother had bought one for each of her grandchildren as a piece of Switzerland to take back to Italy.

We left late at night, after drinking a high-percentage kirsch, a Swiss cherry brandy, which was supposed to render the mass of gobbled-up melted cheese more digestible. Katrin accompanied us to the door, and we stampeded back to our chalet, leaving tracks in the fresh snow. I looked back to see Katrin still standing in front of her chalet, waiting for the last of our silhouettes to disappear into the winter night. The moon was showing us the way, the kids had a snowball fight with their uncles and my back felt okay for the first time in weeks. It was cold and I knotted my daughter's Glarner Tüechli tighter. Bright red like a Swiss passport, the handkerchief with the imported paisley design had become the epitome of Swissness. Sold as a souvenir, it was worn around the neck or as a bandana by locals, tourists, mountaineers and even dogs—and most proudly, by patriots and xenophobes who were rising again to fiercely protect our customs and country from any foreign influence.

***

Fola and Precious's permits of stay were ready for pickup when I got back from our skiing holiday. The immigration officer was less hostile this time but repeated again that if it had been up to him, he wouldn't have let them back into the project. Luckily, the prefecture had the final say in the matter. I let him huff and puff for a bit and decided not to waste energy on arguing with him. I had lived in Italy for long enough to know that it was a nightmare to have an enemy behind a public desk. It was always best to keep up the friendliness with the narrow-minded officers of the government. Probably not just in Italy.

Fola and Precious signed the permits of stay and put them in their purses.

"Mum, will we get our pocket money now?" Precious asked, as soon as we left the office.

"Yes, but not for the days you stayed at the house before you were officially accepted back into the project. And I will detract the money for your train tickets from your pocket money."

"Mum, why?" Precious raised her voice.

"Because I don't intend to pay for your trips if you can't even be bothered to respect your turn cleaning!"

I had wanted to prepare a coffee before taking the girls to the city in the morning. But the stove was in such a deplorable state that I preferred to skip the caffeine. Precious should have cleaned it a few days before. She hardly ever cleaned when it was her turn, which led to a domino effect. Since she hadn't done her share, the next girl wouldn't do hers either, and so on ad infinitum, as the Italian family obviously then cleaned less too. Lesley had run a cleaning business for a few years and managed to keep the situation in check when she was around, but I had little patience for cleaning myself and absolutely hated having long discussions to make sure that everybody followed through with their chores.

This time around, Precious excused herself by saying that there had been no detergent in the house. This was true—the shopping issue had still not been resolved, and I had to explain to Precious that if this happened again, she would just have to make do and clean the stove with water.

"Mum, I understand about the tickets." Fola nodded her head vigorously and the big shiny curls of the wig one of the other girls must have lent her bobbed rhythmically up and down. "I'll be happy to pay you for the tickets as soon as we get our pocket money." It was good to hear that at least Fola saw my point. "But mum, before that, could you lend me some money for a train ticket to Rome. I need to visit somebody, now that I can travel again."

***

Nadia came over for lunch on the last Sunday in February. She had just gotten back from visiting friends and family in South Africa. We had stopped the yoga classes before Christmas and needed to decide whether to take them up again now that she was back.

"Look, we can talk about me volunteering for something else, but the yoga lessons—it just doesn't work. At least not now. And believe me, as a yoga teacher, I really didn't think I'd ever say something like this!"

She was right. There was no point in trying again. I would miss it, though. I had really enjoyed the lessons, once I had learned to block out the resentful looks to my left and right. I opened a bottle of wine to propose a toast to the end of our short-lived project and gave Nadia an update on everything that had happened in the winter, starting with Fola's first phone call and her adventurous return, narrowly followed by Precious's.

"That's crazy!" Nadia exclaimed.

"It was!"

"How is it going now?"

"So-so. Precious picked a fight the other night with Izogie. They never got along, but I hope we'll be able to sort it out."

"A fight? You mean an argument?"

"No, it was the start of a proper fistfight. Hope called me at ten at night and got Izogie to talk to me. I was able to calm her down, but it hadn't been fun."

"Oh, shit. And how's the whole financial situation?"

"Lesley and I still haven't been paid. Teresa keeps avoiding us, and the new charity supposed to step in at the beginning of the year has just informed us that they are not going to make it for the end of February. We're going to be in limbo for another month."

"You should just drop everything. I'm sure they'll figure something out once you're gone."

Sergio nodded in agreement and went down to the garden to get some herbs for the salad and pasta sauce. Until I had some positive news, he preferred not to hear all the details again.

"Sergio seems to agree with me," Nadia said.

"Obviously. But I don't want to give up now. I'm too involved. I like the girls, even if they drive me crazy at times. And there must be something we can do to help interrupt the trafficking, even if it's one step forward, two steps back."

"Did you talk to that organization in Rome again?"

"Be Free?"

"Exactly."

"I talked to Francesca, the sociologist I had been in touch with the first time around."

"What did she say?"

"I talked to her after Precious and Fola came back. I thought the fact that they had chosen to return to the house meant that we had established some sort of trust. But nothing much has changed. I have no way of ever knowing whether what I'm being told is true or has just been made up. Francesca said that her experience is similar. She supports a lot of young Nigerian women at the deportation center near Rome. And it's often only then, when everything else has failed, that they disclose what's really going on."

"And how is Lesley holding up in all of this?" Nadia asked.

"I don't know how she's doing it. I'd go nuts if I were her. She traveled with her seventy-five-year-old mother to Catanzaro last week for a court hearing. When they turned up after the fourteen-hour trip, they were told that the judge had to postpone the hearing. No excuse, no prior notice, just a note with the date for the next appointment in two months' time."

"That's incredible! Can they actually do that?"

"They've done it several times so far. Lesley's crazy husband is a small fish, but his grandfather was a big-shot politician. And he may have some Mafia connections too. Most of the social workers who have started looking at her case have let it drop like a hot potato."

"You guys really need some good news soon." Nadia grabbed the bottle to refill our glasses, and I got up to start the pasta sauce.

"Ah, wait, there's something else," I said. "Hope was pregnant."

"Hope was pregnant? Holy shit! *When*? What happened?"

"She had an abortion a month ago."

"Do you know who the father was?"

Sergio walked back into the kitchen just when Nadia asked

the question.

"Not me," he answered.

I was dumbstruck for a moment, before I collapsed into a hysteric fit of laughter. Sergio was standing in the middle of the room in a striped apron, with both hands raised high in the air—arugula leaves in one and rosemary sprigs in the other—to underline his innocence. Nadia was laughing tears and tried in vain to scrub off the red wine that she had spilled on the tablecloth.

I was called back to reason by the pungent scent of burnt garlic, which, reduced to tiny black crumbs, kept sizzling away for my pasta sauce. I turned off the gas, opened the French doors as wide as possible and, still smiling at the absurdity of it all, started to peel a new clove of garlic. I had been sure that we had hit rock bottom during the winter, but actually—things could have been a lot worse.

IV

Spring

17

In accordance with the change of season, the atmosphere at the townhouse in Dogana had become lighter and more relaxed by the end of March. After a long house hunt, Anna and her kids had at last found an affordable apartment to rent from the beginning of May. Once they left, three more bedrooms could be taken up by refugees. This would generate more income for the charity stepping in and render the refugee home financially self-supporting. The thirty-five euros the government paid organizations per refugee per day was a fair compensation; in fact, more and more hotels and farm stays were popping up that, after difficult years in tourism, were opening their structures to refugees instead.

I hadn't had much success with my various educational projects, but the language lessons were finally rolling again. During the winter, the girls' latest Italian teacher, a friendly woman from a nearby village who had replaced Martina, had had an accident on the icy road to Dogana. After nearly two months of recovery, she was back for the regular two lessons a week. And through an acquaintance, I had met Giulia, a young woman from the village who volunteered to take on the literacy classes with Izogie, Fola and Rita. Giulia got along with the girls right away, and especially Izogie kept making progress. I had worried that the girls' dislike for Dogana could lead to friction with their new literacy teacher, but Giulia turned out to be the person to properly understand them. She had grown up in the Tuscan hinterland and knew about the limited and lackluster opportunities for young women whose main interests weren't in farming, soccer or endless rounds of aperitifs at the local bar.

The most exciting news the warmer season brought was that Joyce had found a job. We were sitting in the March sun on the terrace when she told me about her future as a babysitter in Rome.

"I'll work for a Nigerian family with two small kids."

"How did you find them?"

"Through a friend I met on Facebook. She says I'll be able to stay with the family. They have a sofa bed in the living room."

"You haven't met the family yet?"

"No, but we talked on the phone."

"And you're sure they truly are a family looking for a babysitter?"

"Yes, why would they have asked me otherwise?"

"I just don't want you to be tricked into anything else."

"Mum!" Joyce looked at me and laughed. "My friend knows this family well!"

"Fine. If you're sure that everything is kosher... When are you supposed to start?"

"As soon as possible, but I thought it might be better if I waited 'til I have seen the commission."

"Don't. They might end up giving the job to somebody else. For all we know, you might have to wait several more months for your appointment."

"I just don't want to lose my chance to see the commission in Florence. I've been waiting for this appointment for so long now. In Rome, I might have to start all over again."

Joyce, Hope, Izogie, Precious and Fola had arrived in Italy

in July. Eight months later, they still had not received their appointment with the human rights commission in Florence. And unless the outcome of the hearing was positive, the waiting wouldn't finish then. Rita had arrived in Italy half a year before the other girls and had already had her hearing in Florence. Her asylum request had been rejected, and she now had a lawyer, who had lodged an appeal for her. This meant waiting again. Easily for another year, or maybe even two. Three appeals could be lodged, and a lot of time passed between each of them.

"Joyce, think of Rita. Most asylum requests from Nigerians were rejected last year. I know you hope yours won't be, but sitting here waiting for your appointment won't change that. You have a work permit, so take advantage of the job in Rome. The quicker you are out of here, the better for you."

The following weekend, Joyce traveled to Rome to meet the family. She came back to Dogana looking happy and ready to move on. The prospect of leaving the refugee home had turned the dejected and sulky Joyce I had been struggling with all winter into the upbeat and friendly young woman that she must have been before leaving Nigeria. The horrific trip to Europe and the months, or years, spent killing time in a refugee home could wear down the most energetic and proactive twenty-year-old. The Italian government urgently needed to increase staff at the territorial commissions to speed up the procedure and shorten the waiting time in the shelters. This wouldn't just improve the psychological and physical well-being of the asylum seekers but also save Italy's taxpayers a lot of money.

The warmer temperatures and Joyce's job offer motivated the other girls. Hope asked for a special permit to stay in Pisa for more than five days for a work trial at a restaurant near the station. And Rita needed extra time in Rome, where a friend of hers worked as a cleaner in a business that was looking for new staff. Rita was good-natured and fun to be with, but I definitely couldn't see her as a cleaner. She did her share in the house but otherwise moved as little as possible. Nevertheless, it was worth a try.

***

In mid-March, I received a phone call from Teresa. I stared at the phone for a while, surprised to see her number and tempted to emulate Teresa's own tactic of just letting it ring. But in the end, curiosity got the better of me: After all the hiding behind her fancy new desk, what could she want?

It turned out to be a question of politics. Dogana's town council had a meeting coming up with the prefect and Teresa was hoping to find a few refugees who wanted to take part in it. The prefect's visit was set for March 21, which happened to be the International Day for the Elimination of Racial Discrimination. The council had decided to decorate the town hall with yellow flowers for the event (the color usually used in antiracism demonstrations in Italy), and Teresa had proposed to ask a group of refugees whether they'd like to give a little speech about their experience at the shelters in Tuscany.

I couldn't believe Teresa had the guts to call me for this. She had kept avoiding us for the last eight months, and now that she needed to look good in front of the prefect, she suddenly showed interest in our work and the well-being of the girls. I should have told her to screw off, but her brazenness had caught me off guard. Besides, it really was up to the girls to decide. Izogie and Hope liked the idea and started to prepare a little speech with Giulia and me. Izogie was too shy in the end and felt her language skills weren't good enough to speak in front of a crowd. Hope was nervous too, but did a good job. She gave the prefect and the council a summary of her difficult trip to Europe, the time she spent in Dogana and her hope to study nursing one day to help people in need (a dream that had been born during her hospital visits for the abortion, a detail we decided didn't need mentioning in front of the prefect).

After Hope's speech, Teresa got up to tell the prefect about our work at the refugee home. Prior to the meeting, Teresa had asked me for an email update of all the activities that had been organized for the girls and now outlined them to the assembly.

"Our refugee home in Dogana doesn't just offer Italian lessons. We also organize yoga and literacy classes. We have set up a computer course for our guests during the last months and we are planning..."

We? Who was "we"?

I looked around the town hall and saw the prefect and the audience nod in approval of all the fine activities Teresa and her—apparently—tight-knit team had organized. The longer she talked about the things "we" had done, the more I wondered whether she would also have used the majestic plural if Lesley and I, and the volunteers helping out at the refugee home, had totally screwed up. Probably not. No doubt, Teresa was destined for a long political career.

***

I met Teresa again a few days later, during a meeting at the refugee home with Pio, Domenico and Maria. Pio had organized the meeting to shed some light on Lesley's and my agreements with Teresa and our missing work contracts. After the experience at the town hall, I was prepared for the worst, but Teresa surprised me by confirming the terms of our spoken agreements with her exactly as Lesley and I had already laid them out to the new organization. It was good to see that Teresa seemed to have retained some of the sense of responsibility and integrity that I had admired her for when I started working at the charity years before. But I still had no idea why she had changed so much in the meantime. My guesses ran the gamut from an undeclared nervous breakdown to an undetected brain tumor that was slowly eating away her best personality traits.

"And in regard to the outstanding wages, I had told Lesley and Katja in the past that they would be paid once the prefecture sent the money for the running of the refugee home."

"It's just that the money never arrived—" I said.

"It has arrived," Domenico interrupted, "but I'm sorry to say that we had to pay more urgent things first."

"Like what? What is more important than paying the people who have been doing all the work without seeing a penny?"

"The suppliers of the women's shelter, which had not been paid for months either. If the suppliers turn off the lights and gas, we'll have to close the women's shelter in the countryside, and a lot of families who were running from domestic violence will be chucked out into the street."

Pio and Domenico had decided to use the money the prefecture had paid for the running of the refugee home in Dogana (and hence for Lesley's and my wages) to stuff the holes in the finances of the women's shelter. It was a murky practice, but I knew the women who were living there. I had worked with their kids. Of course I didn't want them to be thrown out of their home so that I could get paid.

"Anyway, it's good to know what your agreements were," Pio said. "Teresa, could you prepare two letters that state in writing what we've just talked about? We'll need these to make sure Lesley and Katja's wages can be paid once the charity is financially stable again."

"Absolutely, I'll prepare them this week."

Teresa stopped working for the charity by the end of March, and Lesley and I would never get to see those letters, which were meant to substitute for our missing work contracts. Each time I went back to the town hall to ask Teresa about them, she would insist that she had sent the letters as promised to the board of the charity, and the board of the charity would insist that they had never received them. It was Italy at its best.

By the end of the same week, I had another meeting with Pio, Domenico and Maria. This time without Teresa but with Lesley, who was back from visiting her children. After three months' delay, the new organization was at last ready to take over. Vera made coffee, and Pio, Maria, Domenico, Lesley and I sat around the table and exchanged some pleasantries before we got down to business.

Pio opened the meeting by explaining that Maria would coordinate the work of the various shelters their charity would be in charge of. She was going to be the person Lesley and I would have to report to. Maria took over from Pio and talked about the importance of work schedules, a structured daily routine and a clear outline of the staff's responsibilities. She wanted to talk to Lesley and me in detail to find out how we had organized the work so far. She started to ask Lesley a few questions about her personal situation, and I went into the kitchen to get the coffee. When I returned with the coffeepot and five espresso cups, I was surprised to find Lesley sitting under fire from Maria.

"So you have been living here for how long?"

"Eight months."

"Eight months? That's quite a long time. Don't you think it's time you became independent and found an apartment for you and your mum to live in?"

I started to pour the coffee into the cups and wondered what I had missed. I had had several conversations with Maria and liked her. She was very loquacious and often ended up using ten minutes for things that could have been said in two, but she had a good sense of humor, lots of experience and seemed to do a great job at the refugee home she was already in charge of. I had no idea why she felt she needed to attack Lesley like this, instead of thanking her for all the work she had done.

"I *am* looking for an apartment," Lesley said. "I made a request at the town hall for a social housing apartment. Teresa can confirm this. She helped me with the paper work last autumn."

"That's fine, but I can't see why you're not looking for other options." Maria leaned over the table, intently focusing on Lesley like an eagle on its prey. "Just because you made a request, doesn't mean you'll get the apartment. You'll have to get out there and look for other options. You can't expect to live here forever with your mum. You have to be more proactive."

"*Proactive?*" I slammed a half-filled espresso cup back onto its saucer and fumed at Maria.

"I'm just saying, it's important for Lesley to get out there and—"

"You know what's important for Lesley? To get paid! P-A-I-D. Paid for the work she's been doing for the last eight months!"

Maria leaned back in her chair and stirred some sugar in her coffee. "I wasn't aware the charity owed Lesley money. I thought you were both doing voluntary work."

"Voluntary work?" I couldn't believe it. Lesley and I had talked about all of this with Maria in January. "What about our meeting in that gynecologist's waiting room? I'm sure each patient listening in on our heated conversation remembers that running this home wasn't supposed to be voluntary work!"

"That's right, yes. Sorry, I didn't mean to—"

"If you want to talk about being proactive, than please first start off by being proactive yourself. We told Teresa last November that things weren't working here. Next thing I know, you three arrive and promise to step in in January, and four months later, not only has nothing been sorted out, but you have the guts to come up here and accuse Lesley of being, what—lazy?"

"Now, now," Pio intervened from the head of the table, "let's calm down everybody. Let's calm down and please remember that this whole situation isn't easy for us either. We had no idea what we were getting ourselves into. We are putting in a lot of extra hours too, and we only do this out of respect for Don Vito. You know that we hold the charity's founder in the highest regard. He has ended up trusting the wrong people, and we're trying to sort things out for him. And yes, we obviously think you need to be paid for your work. That's why we organized the meeting with Teresa at the beginning of this week."

"Exactly!" Maria added. "And I really didn't want to offend you. It's really hard to keep track of everything at the moment. The charity is in such a dire state, we have to pick up all the slack Teresa left behind."

Pio and Domenico nodded in agreement.

"So let's all take a deep breath and start again," Pio said. "First, I really want to thank you two for all the work you've done here during the last months. We all agree that it's absolutely unprofessional that you were left to look after this refugee home without a proper contract and without being paid. I'm sure Domenico can confirm this."

"Absolutely. I'm appalled by the way things have been handled so far." Domenico was in charge of the administration of the two charities Don Vito had founded in our province: the one Pio was running and the one they were sorting out after Teresa had screwed up. "It's mandatory in our organization that all employees start work with a detailed contract that lists everybody's rights and responsibilities."

"I can attest to that," Maria said, while topping up her espresso cup. "I've been working with Pio and Domenico for years now and can assure you that they handle everything very professionally. I totally understand what you must be going through. I have had my share of bad experiences with badly run charities, but that's not how we do things. As you know, we have sound experience in running refugee homes, and I'm sure you'll see that things will run smoothly once we take over here in May."

"In May?" Lesley and I asked simultaneously.

Pio cleared his throat before answering. "Yes, that's why we're here today. For legal reasons, our organization can only step in at the refugee home in Dogana from the beginning of May."

"But what about April?" Lesley asked. "We're—"

Pio stopped her with a hand gesture. "I know this isn't ideal, but we're legally bound. The prefecture renews the contracts with the associations running the refugee homes only on the first of May. This gives us, however, the whole month of April to settle things and make sure we're starting on the right foot together in May. Just like you, we can't wait to make a fresh start and leave this mess behind us."

"But what are Lesley and I supposed to do in April?"

Nobody answered. Maria looked at her notes, Domenico typed something into his phone and Pio stirred a spoonful of sugar into his topped-up espresso cup.

"You expect us to keep going like this for yet another month?"

Lesley asked.

"As I said, it's not ideal, but sadly, there is nothing we can do about this." Pio ruffled his scanty hair and looked extremely sorry. "But it's only for one more month."

"So the important thing to remember," Domenico added, looking up from his phone, "is that all the rooms in the house need to be freed up for refugees. It won't be financially feasible for us to keep going like this. As soon as the Italian family moves out, we'll make sure their beds are taken. Since this home was set up for women only, but few female refugees are arriving at the moment, we might transfer the Nigerian women who are staying at our refugee home to yours. We won't have a problem filling their beds, considering arrivals are already peaking again in Sicily."

"We don't have time to talk everything through now," Pio cut in. "We have another meeting at the women's shelter, where the situation is even more complicated than here, and we're already running half an hour late. We'll be back next month to talk about the details of your contract. In the meantime, please remember that we really appreciate everything you're doing here."

Pio, Domenico and Maria left in a hurry, and Lesley and I sat at the table dumbfounded, staring at their empty espresso cups. Another month and nothing had been sorted out. Again.

"Thanks for speaking up for me," Lesley said.

"I still can't believe it. What was she thinking? And they criticize Teresa for not supplying us with a contract, but at the same time, they don't have a problem with telling us to keep working like this?"

"It's crazy. And this Maria really seems to have a problem with me. But I actually can't sit around here waiting to be paid. I have a hearing coming up in April in Catanzaro, and I've spent all my savings on traveling back and forth to see my kids. I hope I get this job at the hotel for the season. I don't know what to do otherwise."

Unlike what Maria had suggested, Lesley hadn't been looking just for an apartment to move into but also for a new job that would allow her and her mum to move out. She had worked under the table as a cleaner and maid at a luxury hotel nearby. The owners called Lesley whenever they had a wedding or big event, and had promised her a proper contract from the start of the new season. But even though they ran a fancy hotel, the aristocratic Italian owners used the same strategy as the charity we were working for. Each time Lesley asked for the details of her contract, the couple answered that they weren't ready yet. I wasn't surprised. The hotel had an awful reputation among the locals in our area. The owners were known to put on their best smile for the super wealthy people who had the cash to get married at their castle, and then turned around to treat their underpaid staff appallingly. It was the Tuscany that turned my guts.

"Look," I said, "I can handle this on my own for a month. The girls are often away on the weekends anyway. You stay with your friends down south, save the money for the train tickets, and I'll keep you updated on how things proceed here. I'll call your mum on the days I'm not at the house before I send the daily info to the prefecture. She can tell me if one of the girls went away without telling me."

"You're sure?"

"Absolutely. The girls are doing fine at the moment. We'll manage."

"Okay, if you think so." Lesley got up to collect the empty espresso cups and take them to the kitchen. She turned around before she reached the door. "I'm never sure what goes through these girls' heads. Let's hope this isn't just the calm before the storm."

"I'm sure it isn't."

***

Lesley left that afternoon, and two days later, lightning struck. Anna was the first one to call me at eleven o'clock on Sunday night. I could hardly hear her anxious voice among all the shouting that was taking place on her side of the phone.

"Anna, what the hell is going on?"

"Izogie and Rita are fighting. It's scary. They won't stop shouting."

"Have you tried to calm them down? Is Lesley's mum nearby?"

"We all tried. Hope and Precious too. But Izogie is totally out of control. She's threatening Rita with a broken beer bottle. We don't know what to do!"

"Stay in your rooms. I'm calling the police."

There had been several loud arguments in the house. Some of them frightening mostly because of the level of noise involved, but there had never been any violence before. I called the carabinieri and heard back from them half an hour after their arrival at the house. I had already talked to Hope and Lesley's mum in the meantime and was relieved to hear some laughter in the background when I was talking to the police officer in charge.

"We calmed them down. It's not clear who started it, but Rita is definitely worse off. She's got a wound on her chest and must have been punched in the eye."

"Shall I call a doctor?"

"We already tried to, but Rita doesn't want to hear of it. And she doesn't want to denounce the girl who attacked her."

"She doesn't want any trouble with the immigration office."

"Exactly. But we warned them. They'll be in trouble if this happens again. It looks like they got the message."

I knew the police officer I was talking to from the time our house had been broken into. He used to live in our village and had been extremely friendly and helpful then too.

"Thanks so much, Dante. I'll be at the house tomorrow and will try to figure out what happened."

"Good luck. There is always trouble if too many women share a house."

"You would know!"

"Yep. That's why I'm always armed!" Dante was the only man in a household of women. His wife and daughters definitely didn't seem to be the fistfighting type, but I was relieved that he viewed the situation with a sense of humor.

But Sergio didn't.

"It's one in the morning. And it's time you make a decision."

"I know."

He turned over and switched off the light.

I went into the kitchen, pulled out my laptop and put the kettle on, while wondering what had gotten into Izogie. She was short-tempered but normally calmed down as quickly as she ignited. I prepared myself a herbal tea and started to draft the email that I planned to send to Pio first thing in the morning.

18

March 30, 2015

Dear Pio, Maria and Domenico,

I received a phone call from Anna late last night. Izogie and Rita were fighting, and Anna was worried about the safety of the people in the house. I decided to call the police after hearing that Izogie was threatening Rita with a broken bottle. There have been other agitated discussions in the house, but they never escalated like this before.

With the arrival of the police, the situation calmed down quickly. The police offered to call a doctor—Rita has a black eye and several bruises—but she insisted that this wasn't necessary. She also declined reporting Izogie for the aggression.

Please let me know how you deal with incidents like these at your refugee home and how you report them to the prefecture. Considering that I operate in total limbo without a contract, the question is also whether I have the authority to report the incident in the first place.

In light of what happened last night, we'll also have to evaluate whether, once the Italian family has moved out, it's a good idea to have even more young Nigerian women—most of them caught in very difficult and complex situations—sharing the rooms at the house. It might be worth changing the setup so that the home can also take in male refugees in the future. That said, unless I receive a proper contract for the month of April, and the prospect of being regularly paid for my work, I will no longer be available to take care of the refugee home.

I await your reply,
Katja

***

Maria called me the same day and promised they'd find a way to provide a work contract for me for the month of April.

"I'm sorry that I'm only calling now. We had to deal with an emergency at our own refugee home today. People are just fed up with the long waits and have started taking it out on us. Anyway, we saw your email and agree that your contract is a priority. Pio and Domenico actually have a meeting coming up with the board of your charity. They will explain the situation and make sure that the board understands the difficult situation you're dealing with."

Domenico called me a couple of days later to confirm that the board had agreed to hire me until their organization stepped in. I met him at the end of the week on the terrace of Dogana's village bar to sign the contract. I ordered an aperitif and read through the document.

"Five hundred euros?"

"Yes, that's all we could get out of them."

"And what happens after this contract ends on April 30?"

"You'll have a contract with our organization from the first of May."

"You're really sure about that? No offense, but I've been hearing you saying this for several months now."

"We're a hundred percent sure this time around. So from the first of May, you'll get a different contract, since you'll be working for our charity from then on."

I signed the paper work and sipped my aperitif. The view over the green valley, the warm spring weather and a contract—things were looking up at last. But Domenico didn't look good at all. He had dark circles under his eyes, and sudden coughing fits kept interrupting our conversation.

"You look tired," I said. "What's going on?"

"Too much work. I have not had a moment during the last months. The more we dig in, the more nightmares we unearth."

"Nightmares because of Teresa's handling of the charity?"

Domenico took a sip of his beer and didn't answer. I couldn't tell whether he was too annoyed to tell me about it or he had been instructed not to talk to anybody about the financial and administrative mess they were uncovering. Whatever the reason, I was tired of being kept in the dark.

"Teresa told me that she invested a lot of her own money during the last year to keep the women's shelter afloat. Is that true?"

"It may be. I don't know."

"From what she told me, this situation emerged because the Italian government is no longer able to pay the subsidies for the women and children who are staying at the women's shelter. She said social services were always slow to pay, but things had never been as bad as they are now."

"She said that?" Domenico shook his head. "Obviously, if you don't send the invoices and requested documentation to the social security office, the government can't pay, even if it wanted to."

"She didn't send the invoices?"

"Exactly."

"And what about the refugee home?"

"Same thing. I had to remind her at least three times to finally send off the invoice to the prefecture."

"Am I understanding this right? Teresa told Lesley and me that she'd pay our outstanding wages as soon as the money from the prefecture arrived but at the same time never actually bothered to send them the invoice?"

"When did she tell you that?"

"Last December."

Domenico shook his head and finished his beer.

"So if Teresa just kept covering up her own mistakes, why did nobody intervene? The board of the charity should have noticed ages ago!"

"She did some very good work. Many of the social work practices are very well done. The board trusted her blindly. But anyway, I have to go. We'll talk next week."

"Wait, but what about Lesley?"

"What?"

"I have a contract now, but what about Lesley?"

"Now, that's something else we wanted to talk about with you. We don't think we can hire Lesley—" Domenico couldn't finish the phrase because of a coughing fit.

"Sorry?"

"We won't have enough money to hire both of you."

"I thought we already talked about this!" Domenico and Maria had told me before that for financial reasons they were planning to hire only one person in Dogana. And I had already told them that Lesley and I were happy to job share. Lesley had to travel each week, and I couldn't take on the job on my own. I had other work to look after. Also, having somebody to share ideas and problems with was essential in this job. "As I said, I'm not interested in looking after the refugee home on my own. Lesley and I either share the job, or she's the one you'll have to hire."

"Now, that's not quite how we see it."

"Why, how do you see it?"

"We think you're better prepared for the job. Offering to step back for Lesley is very charitable of you. It's, er, the humanitarian way to think about it, but sadly we have to look at it from the professional side. The refugee home really has to work financially too."

"I'm the first person to agree. The home has to work financially, but that doesn't mean that you can turn your back on the people who picked up the slack while the charity was a mess. Especially not in the case of Lesley, who was actually sent here so that the charity could support her and not the other way around!"

"We don't think she's qualified for the job."

"She's Nigerian. She has lived in Italy for nearly two decades and speaks fluent Italian, English and pidgin. If she isn't qualified to work with these girls, who is?"

***

Back home, I told Sergio about the irregularities the new organization had discovered in Teresa's work. Obviously, behind the facade things hadn't been looking too good for quite a while. I also showed him my new contract, but he wasn't too impressed.

"Interesting, though, isn't it?" Sergio said.

"What?"

"Last week, Pio and Domenico told you that, sadly, there was no way they could help you with a contract for April. And now that you threatened to leave, they were suddenly able to talk to the board of the organization, and voilà, here it is?"

"I thought about that too. But they really *are* under a lot of pressure. As long as I'm going to be paid from now on, I'm fine with that. Now, we just have to make sure that they won't cut off Lesley." It would take several more discussions with the new organization before Lesley was finally granted a temporary contract for her work in Dogana.

"When will they pay you?" Sergio asked.

"Maria told me that their organization always pays by mid-month, latest by the twenty-fifth."

"Now, that's a reason for a party. May 25 it is. I'll make pizza and let's fly in your family too."

"My family? Why?"

"To celebrate all that Italian efficiency: a first paycheck after a mere ten months of work? I'm sure the Swiss will want to party along!"

***

Joyce moved out in the second week of April to start her job as a babysitter in Rome. She sounded cheerful every time I heard from her. She got along well with the couple she stayed with and enjoyed looking after their kids.

But things didn't look quite as good for everybody else. Hope had not gotten the job at the bar in Pisa. The clients were mostly locals, and her Italian hadn't been good enough for her to understand them. And Rita had come back from Rome without a cleaning job. Her Nigerian friend had taken her along for a day, but Rita didn't go back after that. She said it was too hard on her back but nevertheless stayed in Rome for a few more days. I should have asked her to come back earlier, since she was no longer interested in the job, but let it slip for once. She kept wearing her Jackie Kennedy glasses to cover up the black eye from the fight with Izogie. It was clearly not the best outfit to wear when applying for a cleaner's job. Izogie had calmed down, but I still thought it advisable that Rita didn't cross her path for a bit.

In the meantime, Izogie was learning to deal with her anger differently and started to take longs walks to calm down when she was on the brink of losing her temper. Izogie's irascible nature had served her well since she was a teenager. She had lost her parents early and had to look after herself since she was thirteen. She had moved to Benin City from the countryside and worked various jobs in which being able to defend herself with her fists was an important survival tool. But this was no longer the case in our Italian refugee home. If she wanted to stay, she needed to keep her resilience, strong will and sense of humor—the traits that helped her make all the progress with learning to read and write—but let go of her pride.

Precious and Fola had taken to traveling a lot, just like the other girls. I had to constantly remind everybody that they were free to move out if they could find a place to stay. It made no sense to keep the beds for them if they were away a lot. Arrivals in Sicily had continued throughout winter, and with the warmer season, the numbers started to peak again, but the people who had arrived a year or two before were still stuck in the refugee homes.

Fola called me one day from the station after coming back from her second visit to Rome. She had just lost her purse on a bus. She was totally distressed. Her permit of stay and all her money had been in the purse. I told her to calm down and explained that we could ask for a copy of her permit of stay at the immigration office once the original had been reported stolen or lost.

"Mum, I'm not worried about the document. I need the money!"

"The money? How much money did you have in the purse?"

"Two hundred and twelve euros, mum." Fola sniffed into the phone. "I need my money back! Please call the bus company for me. The people here can't help me."

I googled the bus company and found several phone numbers on their website. The first two weren't working anymore, and the third one connected me to a grumpy operator who wasn't in the mood to help. Fortunately, Fola had more luck than me. She ran into Anna's son, who was waiting at the bus stop to get back to Dogana. He talked to the guy at the ticket booth, who was suddenly helpful now that he was talking to an Italian. It turned out that her purse was still on the bus she had been on. She returned overjoyed. Nobody had taken anything. Her permit of stay and money were still in the purse.

"Mum, it's all fine. Michele sorted it out. They didn't understand me at the office."

"I'm happy to hear it, but how come you're back from Rome with two hundred euros in your purse?"

"Mum?"

"The money. Where's it from?"

"My boyfriend gave it to me."

"You have a boyfriend?"

"Yes, mum!" Fola swiped the screen of her new smartphone and showed me a picture of a good-looking young man with dreadlocks.

"Where is he from?"

"From Nigeria. We met on Facebook."

"And he gave you all that money, just like that?"

"Yes, mum."

"And this smartphone too?"

"Yes, mum."

"What does he do?"

"He works."

"What kind of work?"

"I don't know yet, mum. I only just met him."

"You only just met him and he already gave you two hundred euros and a smartphone?"

"Mum, I told you, he's my boyfriend now. We need the phone to talk. And he gave me the money to buy some things and a train ticket for the next time I travel to Rome. He wants to take care of me."

"Sure."

Fola took a step back and scrutinized me, hands on her hips. "Mum, you don't believe me!"

"No, I don't."

"Let me call my boyfriend." Fola started to frantically look for a number on her phone.

"Forget it, Fola."

"Here, mum!"

I waved her phone out of my face. Maybe Fola had a boyfriend. Maybe not. But I sure wouldn't find out by talking to the stranger on the other end of the line. "Just remember that you need to be here for your Italian and literacy lessons. There is no point to you staying at the refugee home if you're not participating in the activities organized for you."

"Mum, I might find a job if I keep going to Rome."

I wondered what kind of job she had in mind. Since she had gotten back from Turin, Fola only wore tight and super short dresses with extremely revealing necklines. She looked sexy but totally out of place in a Tuscan hilltop town. But then, the Italian TV presenters on the programs Anna and one of her daughters watched all day long dressed exactly like her. Perhaps Fola had just chosen the wrong role models. In my opinion, at least.

***

The American journalist I had been in touch with since December had gotten back to Italy in the spring. She emailed me and suggested we meet for lunch in April to discuss work or apprenticeship opportunities for the girls in the hotel industry. It was high time. Hope needed a challenge. She was getting more and more depressed since the job in Pisa had fallen through. She was smart and great with people—if she wanted to. Her computer skills were basic, but she was quick to learn, and the important bit was that she spoke very good English. I had spent a season working at a hotel reception in Montalcino when I first arrived in Italy. I could hardly understand a thing my Tuscan boss told me, but it didn't matter much since most clients were English speakers anyway, and by the end of the season, I had learned a lot of Italian by jumping into the deep end. In the same way, any real-life practice and on-the-job learning would be better for Hope than all the Italian lessons I could possibly organize in Dogana.

I told the girls about my upcoming meeting, but the journalist had—like everybody else in the Western world—a busy schedule. She had to cancel our appointment because of a sudden deadline at work but promised to get back to me. It was pure irony. I was working with people in their early twenties doomed to spend their best years sitting around waiting for documents and commission appointments, while all my fortysomething friends and acquaintances were battling too much stress and pressure in their jobs and a constant feeling that they never had enough time for their personal lives. And if they had, the days off weren't the relaxing oasis they were yearning for but minefields scattered with aging parents, challenging children or difficult relationships. I desperately wished for a magic wand to sort things out and split up everything more evenly. But it turned out that I would need that wand to resolve a much more troubling matter.

19

On April 14, a migrant boat sank in the Mediterranean. The Italian navy saved 142 lives eighty nautical miles south of Lampedusa. An estimated 400 people died. A second boat capsized on April 18, just outside of Libyan waters. In the worst ship disaster of its kind, 800 people drowned and 27 survived. The two tragedies called Europe back to a sense of responsibility it didn't want. But blaming Italy for lack of border controls and helping migrants in distress wouldn't make the problem go away.

A social worker from the emergency reception center in the city called me five days after the first boat sank to tell us that one of the survivors, a twenty-one-year-old woman from the Gambia, would be referred to the refugee home in Dogana later that same day. Ida had been traveling the "back way," the Western Sahara route that takes migrants from the tiny country on Africa's western coast via Senegal, Mauritania, Mali, Burkina Faso and Niger to Libya. She had been with her husband, brother and sister-in-law. All of them had drowned when the boat went down. The social worker added that Ida was absolutely lovely, and she hoped I would take good care of her.

I put down the phone wondering what taking good care looked like in a case like this. 1,200 people—more than double the population of the village I lived in—had lost their lives in the Mediterranean just days ago. I expected Ida to be in a state of shock and utter desolation, and felt just as relieved that I could actually do something for a survivor of the tragedy, as I was clueless about how to best approach the situation.

I decided to consult Aziz, the young man who had come by our home a few months earlier to ask for Sergio's winter jackets. Aziz and several of his friends, who all lived at the refugee home in our village, were the only Gambians I knew. Aziz was trying hard to fight the ennui and lingering depression refugees fall prey to by building an improvised business. He had started off by traveling to Tuscany's refugee homes to sell Italian SIM cards to people who had just arrived, and I had had the brilliant and extremely shortsighted idea of suggesting Aziz start importing African wax prints. I promised to find customers among my friends who loved the fabrics' colorful geometric patterns just as much as I did. Aziz could make some money, and at the same time, we would be supporting the workers of the African textile industry. But the day I unwrapped the parcel with material Aziz's aunt had bought in the market in Banjul, I also discovered that the exuberant prints had been produced in Europe and could be ordered directly from the Netherlands without the African detour. The Dutch had been more successful in surviving the decline of the European textile industry than the businesses in the Swiss mountain valley where I holidayed. The Dutch wax prints were in as high demand as ever in West Africa, and their fiercest competitors for a slice of the market were not the local industries but the cheaper Chinese imports.

I called Aziz to tell him about Ida and the latest boat disasters.

"We have seen the news about the boats," he said. "She is very lucky to be alive. Let me know what we can do."

"Thanks, Aziz. I'll be in touch as soon as I know more."

I drove to the house and asked Izogie to help me prepare a bed for our new guest. The Italian family hadn't moved out yet, but two tiny rooms in the basement had been freed up by the local doctor who had used them as a temporary studio and waiting room twice a week. Fola had already turned one into a bedroom, and we moved a mattress into the other. I told the girls about Ida. They had also heard about the two boats that had gone down, but they didn't say much. Empathy wasn't their strong suit. I didn't know whether the absence of it was because of a difficult upbringing or the atrocities they encountered in the eye-for-an-eye world of Libya's ghettos, and I had gotten tired of trying to find out.

Two operators of the women's shelter drove Ida to Dogana, and the first thing I noticed when she got out of the car was her smile. A warm and wide smile set in a beautiful deep-black face. It made me falter for a moment—I had been prepared for tears, breakdowns and supportive hugs but definitely not for a radiant smile. I collected myself, took Ida's small bag and accompanied her along the steep alley leading up to the house.

"Are there any Gambians staying here?" was the first thing she asked when we walked into the house, followed right after by "I need to get to Germany."

I showed Ida around the house and explained why she couldn't travel on to Germany. I also told her about the young men from the Gambia who were staying at the refugee home in my village. The Italian family was packing up and getting ready for their move. Ida kept smiling and greeted everybody. Fola offered her a plate of jollof rice. She ate a few bites but wasn't really hungry. I asked her whether she'd like to lie down.

"No, mum. I can't sleep. But please let me meet your friends from Gambia."

I called Aziz and drove back home with Ida. She sat on a bench under an olive tree while I made coffee and tea. Aziz arrived shortly after with two of his friends and joined her at the table in the grove. The four of them started to talk in Wolof, and from time to time, their conversation was interrupted by the ringing of Ida's phone.

Aziz explained, "It's people calling her to find out about their relatives."

"Relatives who were on the boat?"

"Exactly. They hope she might know what happened to them."

"How did they get the number? This isn't her phone." Ida was using the cell phone the reception center in the city kept for people who needed to get in touch with their families. I had bought some credit for her, but the social worker told me that she needed the phone back as soon as there were new arrivals.

"This kind of news travels fast. She called somebody from this phone, and that person must have passed on the news that a survivor can be reached at this number."

I looked at Ida, who was still on the phone. She was smiling and kept answering the questions of all the people who had managed to get her number and explained every time anew what had happened on the boat before her family had drowned, just like the parents, siblings, children or friends the callers were desperately looking for.

"Has Ida told you about Germany?" Aziz asked.

"Yes, she has," I said.

"She has a cousin there."

"I know. She called her from my phone."

"She is desperate to go and stay with her."

"She can't. At least not according to the Dublin Regulation. The European Union allows family reunifications for couples and parents and their minor children. A cousin isn't a close enough relationship. And even if it was, she doesn't have any documents that can prove that they're relatives."

"This cousin is the only person she has."

"I'm trying to find a refugee home for her with women from Gambia. Hopefully, we'll manage to find one somewhere close by so we can keep giving her a hand."

"You know I have seen a lot." Aziz shook his head, and I thought of the long scar he had shown Sergio and me during one of his visits. He had been shot by a teenage sniper in Tripoli. The young Libyan was sitting at a window with a rifle and aimed at every black person that came through his street. Aziz had been lucky to survive. He had heard from a doctor at the improvised hospital friends had carried him to that others hadn't. "I've seen a lot of trouble, but you know this... this is not easy."

Ida stayed for dinner at our place. I prepared fried vegetables and steamed rice—something I hoped Ida would like—but she ate little and burped a lot. The kids watched Sergio and me, waiting for a reaction from us to all her belching.

"Sorry, the water," Ida said after another burp. "I've swallowed so much water. It's still coming up. The people who took us to Sicily told me it will take awhile."

I drove Ida back to the house in Dogana after dinner. Her room looked nice. Izogie had found an extra pillow and a little table and lamp, which she had installed next to Ida's bed.

I said good night and went back home.

***

Ida called me shortly after I had gone to bed.

"Mum, I hear voices."

"Is it the Nigerian girls? Are they fighting?"

"No, no fighting. Just voices."

"I'm sorry, the girls can be rather loud at times."

"I know, mum. I had a Nigerian friend in Libya. They are always loud, but this is worse."

"Okay, let me check what's going on."

I called Vera, who had already been asleep. Were there any problems in the house? Were the girls fighting again? Vera hadn't heard anything. She got up to check and called me back to say that everything was quiet in the house.

The next day, I drove back to Dogana first thing in the morning. Ida was in the bathroom. Fola had told me she had walked into her room in the middle of the night and asked whether she could stay with her.

"Where did she sleep?" There was only one bed in Fola's room.

"On the floor. You know the carpet I have taken down from the attic? She slept on it.

But she kept waking me up."

Ida opened the bathroom door and smiled at us.

"How are you?" I asked.

"Not so bad, but I couldn't sleep, mum. I heard voices the whole night."

"Vera told me the girls were in bed early last night. Perhaps you heard the voices of the villagers passing by in the alleyway?"

"No, mum, the voices were in my room. I asked this girl whether I could stay with her. But I couldn't sleep much, even then."

Ida got ready and I did a couple of things in the house before we drove to my village for her to meet with Aziz and his friends again.

"Mum, have you thought about what I told you yesterday?" she asked when we got into the car.

"I have... I think you really need to talk this through with Aziz again."

Ida had been clear from the first minute. She wouldn't stay. She couldn't stay. She wanted to reach the one person in Europe who had known her before the tragedy and who would understand her without the need for words. I understood but worried that she wouldn't make it past the border controls and wanted her to give it some time. I could help her in Tuscany, but she couldn't come back if she was stopped while illegally crossing the Swiss or German borders.

"The prefecture will let me know today whether there are any shelters in this part of Tuscany with women from Gambia. And they are also requesting the help of a psychologist for you."

"Mum?"

"A doctor you can talk to. A bit like a good friend or family member who supports you in a difficult situation." I had not had much success so far with my proposals of psychological support with the Nigerian girls, but Ida's case literally screamed for it.

"Mum, I don't want to see a doctor. I just need to be close to my people. Let me call my cousin again today. I want to—"

Our conversation was interrupted by the ringing of Ida's phone. Her number was still making the rounds.

"Malik? No, I'm sorry, I don't think there was a Malik on the boat that pulled me out of the water... There were very few people on it... Yes, I would have met him when we were taken to Sicily."

Malik. I liked the sound of the name. I tried to imagine the face that had belonged to it and wondered whether Malik's lifeless body was trapped in the hulk of the boat on the bottom of the sea or still drifting through the deep blue Mediterranean waters.

In the meantime, Ida kept answering questions and explained once more what had happened on the boat. A ship had been sighted on the horizon. They had no more water on the boat.

People were frightened they wouldn't make it to the coast. Some got up to wave in the hope of grabbing the attention of the passing ship. The man steering their boat shouted to sit down, that the boat would capsize otherwise. But the turmoil was too great, and many had already gotten up and run to one side waving and shouting. The boat keeled over only seconds later. Ida had been lucky. She and her family had been sent into the hull at the start of the journey. Like most of the other people, Ida had been sick during the whole trip, but because she was five months pregnant, she was allowed on deck in the end and jumped as soon as the boat keeled over. She lost the baby in the water.

Ida put down the phone.

"It was his mother." Ida shook her head. "She didn't want me to hang up..."

Ida might have been the last person from the boat Malik's mother would ever be able to talk to. The last person who might have heard her son shout for his life.

"The voices, Ida..."

"Mum?"

"The voices you heard last night... Were they real voices or just voices you hear in your head?" I wasn't quite sure how to phrase it. Even if these voices were just in her head, they were real ones, or at least had been a few days earlier.

"It was very loud, mum. People shouted. Everybody shouted for help, or for their family. You see the scratches I have on my cheeks? A man grabbed me to hold on to something and kept pushing me under the water."

I had seen photos of dead bodies in the sea. But I had never stopped to imagine the horror these people must have lived through before they died.

"The man pushing you down—what did you do?"

"I tried to push him away, but he wouldn't let go. I don't know what happened. I think he must have been pulled away by something. I was suddenly on top of the water again and just put up my arms to paddle and kicked with my feet. I can't swim and kept swallowing water, but I told myself, 'Keep doing it, keep doing it...' I was feeling tired, though. Very tired. And I suddenly realized that it was very quiet. There were no more voices, mum... It was dark and very quiet... I was too tired to continue. I thought about my little sister in Gambia. She is only ten. She would never know how I died."

"But you didn't die."

"Somebody shouted my name. I had already stopped paddling. I had no more force and didn't want to listen, but she kept shouting."

"Who was it?"

"Namira. We had met in Tripoli. She is Eritrean. We had spent a lot of time chatting before getting on the boat. The Italians had already pulled her out. She kept shouting my name from their boat. I don't know how she could see me, but I started paddling again, until they got to me and pulled me up into the boat. The Italians kept searching. They moved through the bodies, but I was the last one they found alive."

I kept my eyes on the road, relieved that I had to drive. All my supportive hugs and comforting smiles seemed out of place. My own boat rides on the Mediterranean had always included snorkeling stops, plenty of drinking water and refreshing swims. All I could possibly say felt hollow and ridiculous.

"Mum?"

"Yes?"

"I will always thank the Italian people. Allah and the Italian people saved me. But I can't stay in Italy. I don't need a doctor, mum. I need to be with my cousin. I know this is not going to be easy, I know I need to be strong, but please help me be with her."

***

I dropped Ida off at the refugee home in my village. Aziz and his friends were already waiting for her. I asked Aziz to explain again in Wolof that it was difficult to get to Germany. Somebody had to try to reach through the shock and all the pain lurking behind her smile to make sure things wouldn't turn out even worse. Ida's cousin knew of people who had made it over the border easily a few months earlier. Most Syrians and Eritreans knew that they had to hurry up before their fingerprints were taken in Italy. But border controls had intensified with the growing number of refugees arriving on southern Europe's shores, and the European Union insisted that Italy had to follow the Dublin Regulation—register all the arrivals and not let anybody pass through the country's border.

After I dropped Ida off, I went back home to check my email. I had a message from the vice-prefect in my inbox. There were no women from the Gambia in shelters in our area, but he was making sure she'd get the support of a psychologist. I turned on the radio and did some more emailing while listening to the news, which ended with an interview with an aircraft expert. The Germanwings plane crash had happened in the French Alps less than a month before. The expert talked about the support system, helpline numbers and trauma counseling that had been organized for family members and close friends of the 149 people who had been murdered by a suicidal pilot. Lawyers were putting together lawsuits to fight for financial reparations and

Lufthansa, the parent airline, had already paid out fifty thousand euros per victim as an immediate support for the mourning family members.

I thought of Ida, one of the few survivors of a boat disaster in which hundreds had died, who was maintaining on her own an improvised helpline for the families that had lost their loved ones. She wouldn't get a lawyer or any financial help, but she still had a cousin who was sitting two borders farther north, a mere ten-hour train ride from Florence. I turned off the radio and went online to buy a one-way ticket to Karlsruhe in southern Germany.

20

Ida and I were stuck at a bus stop close to Siena's northern freeway entrance. April 25 is Liberation Day, one of Italy's national holidays, and half of the buses connecting Siena to Florence weren't running, even though tourist season was already in full swing. Our driver was standing in the bus doorway, explaining to the throng of travelers outside that there were no free seats. People were already standing in the aisle of the bus when we had left the center of Siena. An elderly passenger started swearing about the state of the local transport system. I wanted to join in but suppressed the urge so as to not risk being thrown off the bus. Our driver made an agitated phone call, and then informed the travelers that the company was about to send a second bus.

"Great," said the man who had loudly blamed Jesus Christ and his saintly mother. "Let's get a move on, then!"

But the bus company had instructed the driver to wait for the second bus, and all the passengers who complained about missing trains or planes couldn't persuade him to call headquarters again. I considered trying to get back to Siena's town center, where I had parked my car, but getting there would easily take more time than waiting for the second bus to arrive. Either way, it looked like Ida wouldn't make the twelve o'clock train from Florence. I had bought the ticket for the train at noon because it included only two connections: one in Milan and one in Zurich.

Ida couldn't read and had never been on a train before. I couldn't help at the borders, but I had at least wanted to make sure that she didn't have to ask her way through too many train stations.

The second bus arrived half an hour later and our Liberation Day convoy started its unhurried journey on the freeway that runs along the hills of the Chianti region. I took in the lovely scenery and silently cursed my friend who had declined to put us up for a night in her apartment in Siena. I had stayed at her place before, when traveling to Switzerland, and sleeping in Siena would have meant that Ida and I could have taken an earlier bus to Florence. It hadn't seemed presumptuous to ask. My friend didn't just own a spacious and beautiful flat close to Piazza del Campo but also constantly divulged messages of love, light and spiritual growth on her Facebook feed. The heartbreaking photo of the dead body of a child drifting in the sea had been one of her latest posts. The little girl, who had traveled on the same boat as Ida, had drowned after the vessel had capsized. But all that online activism was hard work, and my friend felt too stressed out to have Ida and me staying over for the night. I was welcome, though, to sleep at her place on my own when traveling back from Florence... Evidently, the amount of empathy and compassion people displayed on social media wasn't necessarily equal to what they could muster in real life.

I checked the time and suppressed another violent curse.

"Are you okay, mum?" Ida asked.

"Sure," I said, pretending to be at ease, even though I wanted to slap myself for relying on public transport on a national holiday.

Ida turned back to the green hills passing by in front of the window, and I kept silently agonizing about the rest of the day. I doubted Ida was in for a smooth trip if the first leg of the journey had already turned out to be so chaotic. I had followed the news about the situation at Italy's borders closely during the past few days. More and more people were being stopped at the borders with France, Switzerland and Austria. But I didn't want to infect her with my fear; the calmer Ida was when trying to cross, the better.

Our convoy stopped halfway to Florence in a small town close to the freeway. I checked Google Maps and the exact timing on the printout of Ida's ticket. We had a chance of making the train, if the two drivers decided to put the pedal to the metal. I had been on countless crazy bus rides in Italy and had always hoped that, one day, I'd find a driver who wasn't talking on his cell phone while disregarding the speed limit. But alas, I hadn't meant for it to happen on this trip.

"Mum, the national holiday today, what is it about?"

"It's called Liberation Day. It celebrates the end of Nazi occupation in Italy. And it commemorates all the people who fought in the Resistance against the Fascist regime."

"When was that?"

"More than seventy years ago. The Fascists had ruled Italy for two decades before that."

Thankful for the distraction, I told Ida about Benito Mussolini, his racist views and colonial ambitions, and the brutality he and his Blackshirts reserved for political opponents. It was a sketchy summary, lacking accuracy and in-depth analysis, but it kept me from obsessively checking the time and our position on Google Maps.

"So, Mussolini was a dictator?"

"Yes. And the sad thing is that there are still people in Italy who think he was a hero." I had seen cheap stone busts of Mussolini's square head sitting prominently in Italian living rooms and a calendar with excerpts of his most famous speeches hanging over the stove in a Tuscan kitchen—a startling sight, considering Tuscany had been the beating heart of formerly Communist Italy, with Umbria and Emilia-Romagna.

"He sounds like our president in Gambia. Jammeh doesn't accept any political opposition."

"Aziz has told me about him. He sounds like a total nutcase."

I had done some reading up about Yahya Jammeh, who has ruled the Gambia since a coup in 1994. His secret service is known to torture political opponents, while his wife spends the small country's taxes on shopping sprees in the United States, where President Jammeh's family owns some posh real estate. As a result Gambians make up one of the biggest percentages of people arriving from sub-Saharan Africa on Italy's shore, even though the country only has 1.8 million inhabitants.

"Jammeh should make sure Gambians get the right to vote and speak their mind, instead of organizing witch-hunts for homosexuals," I said. In addition to thrashing any opposition, Gambia's president belonged to the frighteningly high number of homophobic African leaders.

"But, mum..."

"Yes?"

"Why are they doing it?"

"Who?"

"These men. Why are they doing it?"

"Doing what?"

"Being together with other men."

"That's life. Men can love men, and women can love women. That's just how it is."

"I don't think it's right, mum. It's not normal."

"Ida!" I didn't want to hear this. Not today, not while crossing my own boundaries to help with her trip to Central Europe. "It *is* normal. I have very good friends who are homosexual, and I can assure you that they are *as normal as you and me!*"

The elderly Tuscan couple on the other side of the aisle bent forward in their seats to follow our conversation. I doubted they understood Ida's or my heavily accented English, but the sound of homosexual was close enough to the Italian word *"omosessuale"* for them to get an idea of the issue we were talking about. Nevermind the sexual orientation of Italy's most venerated fashion designers, the topic still led to raised eyebrows among the general population, and calling somebody a homosexual—especially by using the slang term *"finocchio"*—was still a serious offense.

My phone rang and Sergio interrupted any further discussion. "How is it going?"

"Don't even ask. We are on a jammed bus talking about gay rights, and I don't have a clue whether we'll make it to Florence in time for our train!"

"Your train? I thought you were only taking her to Florence?"

"I meant Ida's train."

"Can't you change her ticket?"

"I can get her a new one if we miss the train at noon, but it will be a much more complicated trip, and it won't go via Zurich." Sergio knew about my Swiss friend who would be waiting for Ida at Zurich's main station to help her change trains. At least, this was the plan if Ida actually managed to make it that far.

Our bus got off the freeway and drove swiftly through the suburbs of Florence.

"We're getting closer. I'll call you later."

Liberation Day had messed up public transport, but the traffic in the city was much less intense than I had expected. We made it to the bus terminal near Santa Maria Novella train station much faster than we would have on a normal working day. We got off the bus, heaved Ida's suitcase out of the luggage compartment and walked across the piazza to the station. Ida looked fashionable and not at all like a refugee who had just been saved from a sinking boat. We had found some nice pieces for her to wear in the stacks of discarded clothes at the house, most of them things the girls had bought and no longer wore. But we had had a hard time finding a pair of shoes that fit her. The ones Ida had arrived with were still in good shape, but no young woman would want to be seen wearing the type of lacquered orthopedic shoes with Velcro fastenings that Ida had been given at the emergency reception center in the city. Fortunately, Rita saved the day after coming back from Rome. She also wore a size 41 and presented Ida with a pair of high-top sneakers that she had just bought in the Eternal City. But the true pièce de résistance was the brown suitcase Ida traveled with. It didn't match her outfit, but I expected an experienced customs officer to recognize its certified Swissness immediately. My mother had bought a couple of the nondescript but practical cases with the loyalty points of one of Switzerland's biggest supermarket chains. She had given one of them to me, and I only realized that at least half of the Swiss population must have used up their loyalty points in exactly the same way when the conveyor belt at Zurich airport kept spitting out brown suitcases that looked just like mine. Ida didn't have the famous red passport to go with Switzerland's most popular luggage, but I hoped that pulling mine would at least help her look as if she might.

We still had time to buy a sandwich and a bottle of water at a small bar, and I tried to give Ida a brief explanation of how train stations functioned while we headed towards our platform.

"See here, the lower numbers are on the left and the highest to the right. That means if your train in Milan leaves, say, from number fifteen, you just follow all the numbers to the right."

"Okay."

"Up to which number are you able to read?"

"I don't know mum."

"Anyway, just ask somebody to read the departures board for you, and once you know the platform number of the train leaving for Zurich, follow to the left or to the right depending on whether the platform you're standing in front of is lower or higher than the one you need to get to."

"Mum?"

My explanation sounded complicated even to me. And I doubted Ida knew how to read numbers. She was so desperate to get to her cousin that she'd probably have told me she was able to fly if I had asked her. We walked along the platform and looked for car number eight. A lineup had already formed at its door, and a family who looked Eritrean to me was waiting to get on the train before us. The parents and their two lovely boys were neatly dressed. They were either residents or tourists visiting Italy, or I hadn't been the only one to come up with the no plastic bags and flip-flops rule. I asked the father whether he could help Ida change trains in Milan and explained that she needed to travel on towards Switzerland.

"I'm sorry, madam, but I'm only helping this woman and her children on the train."

You too, I thought.

We got in after them, found a space for Ida's suitcase and, among a group of Italian travelers, the number of her seat. I hugged her and felt terrible sending her off like this.

"Don't worry mum, I'll be fine. Allah will help me."

"I'm sure he will." I tried not to sound sarcastic, but considering what Ida had already gone through, I supposed it was better not to rely too much on divine intervention.

I overheard somebody speaking in Swiss German behind me and turned around to see a blonde woman a row farther down the aisle talking with two teenagers.

"Are you traveling to Switzerland?" I asked her.

"Yes. Why?" The woman looked at me skeptically, or maybe just surprised by the sudden intrusion. The teenagers were as tall and blond as her. They were probably traveling back home after a family holiday in Florence.

"I'm sorry to bother you with this, but would you mind helping the young lady over there change trains in Milan? She needs to get the connection that will take her to Zurich."

"We're going to Zurich too." The woman leaned forward to get a glimpse of Ida. "What's her name?"

"Ida. Her name is Ida. Thanks so much!"

I dashed back to Ida before getting off to tell her to follow the blonde woman with the two teenagers once she arrived in Milan. I waved until the train was out of sight. Standing on the empty platform, I wondered what to do next. Waiting in Florence until I knew whether Ida had made it over the Swiss border seemed the best option. If she was taken off the train on Switzerland's southern border, I could ask a cousin for help who lived in the vicinity of Chiasso. And if she was stopped on the Italian side, I could still hop on a train to Milan and try to meet her there.

I followed the crowd out of the station and cruised aimlessly through the busy town center until I remembered Amblé, in a small tourist-free square a stone's throw from the Ponte Vecchio. I ordered a coffee and sat in the bar's artfully assembled vintage furniture in the piazza. It was a perfect spring day, but I was too nervous to read the newspaper or enjoy the sun. I checked the time and got up to call Ida. She was traveling with an old phone of ours, and I wanted to remind her that she was getting close to Milan. Ida picked up and reassured me once more that she would follow the Swiss woman and her children.

I kept wandering around Florence until I found myself swallowed up by a massive clog of tourists in the middle of Piazza della Signoria. I made my way to the Gucci museum on the other side of the square to find refuge from the crowd. I bought a ticket and was shown the way to the museum by a tall and friendly black custodian who looked very stylish in his well-cut Gucci suit. I went upstairs and walked around the elegant and near-empty exhibition space.

I was standing in front of a photograph by Irving Penn when I checked my phone and realized that it had no reception behind the thick stone walls of the medieval building. I rushed back downstairs into the entrance hall and saw the missed call from Ida as soon as I got some reception. I called her immediately. She was fine, the train had just left Milan and she was sitting next to the Swiss woman, who asked to talk to me.

"Hi. I'm here with Ida. I have a few questions."

"Sure."

"Ida said you bought her the ticket."

"Yes."

"But the car and seat number indicated on her ticket don't exist."

"They don't exist? They have to. I bought the ticket online from the Swiss railway!"

"I saw that on the printout. We asked the conductor for help, and he said it might be a mistake by the system."

"Is the ticket still valid?"

"Yes, the ticket is still valid, but—"

"Great!"

"But what about the border?"

"The border?"

"Ida told us she is traveling to Germany."

"Yes, she is on her way to Karlsruhe."

"But she doesn't seem to have any documents."

"Right. I mean, no she doesn't."

"No passport, no ID?"

"No, no nothing."

"You know that there are controls at the border?"

"Yes. And, er..."

"What?"

"Look, I'm sorry for pulling you into this, but I didn't know who to ask otherwise."

"Sure. I'm glad you did. Ida told us about the boat disaster while we were waiting for the train. I'm just trying to figure out whether you know about anything else we can do to help. The conductor offered Ida a seat in first class, because of the mistake with her ticket. But I thought the best thing would be to keep her here with me and my children. We're trying to make it look as if we're traveling together."

"Which you really are at this point."

"Exactly. Okay, we'll be in touch after the border."

"Wait! What's your name?"

"Claudia. I'm Claudia."

"Thank you, Claudia. And yes, please let me know what's happening."

My new partner in crime hung up, and I was so relieved to know Ida was in good hands that I started to cry. The custodian who had sent me up the stairs, only to see me running down again, started to glance at me. I nodded in his direction and had

224

the good sense to leave before he had to ask me to.

I walked past the Uffizi Gallery and fought my way through the jammed-up Ponte Vecchio towards Piazza della Passera. I wanted to get to the gelateria in the quiet little square on the other side of the river. I hadn't eaten yet and had to make sure I got a sugar boost. I was standing in front of the counter, ordering a cone of *fior di latte* and mint ice cream, when my phone rang.

"Mum, we're through!" Ida shouted.

"You're through! Wow, already! No controls?"

"Yes, there were controls. Wait, Claudia wants to talk to you."

Claudia said hello. Her voice sounded much less calm than during our conversation less than an hour before.

"What happened?"

"They took lots of people off the train when it stopped at the border. I have no idea why they let Ida stay on. I got up and nestled something in the luggage on top of our seats in the hope that I'd be able to shield her from the customs officers who passed through the train. I have never felt so nervous in my whole life! You wouldn't believe how many people were told to get off."

I thought of the woman and the two small boys we had met at Santa Maria Novella station and wondered whether she and her children were stranded on a platform in Chiasso now.

"Is Ida okay?"

"She is. But I don't think we should let her travel on her own. She needs help at the German border if anything goes wrong."

"You're right."

"Ida told me you have a friend waiting for her in Zurich. Do you think she could travel with her to Karlsruhe?"

"I don't know, but I will ask."

"I can try to help otherwise. I was even thinking about whether it would be better to drive her in my car."

"I had thought about it. But I would stick to the train. With the current situation, I doubt a car with a black person in it would make it past the customs officers without being stopped. And you'd risk being denounced as a people smuggler once they found out that Ida is traveling without documents."

"Okay. But I definitely think we shouldn't leave her on her own."

"Let me call my friend. I will let you know right away."

I walked out of the ice cream shop to dial Alexandra's number, wondering how best to ask her whether she would join a total stranger on a train ride to Germany. I was halfway across the piazza when I heard somebody shout, "Signora, signora!" behind me. I turned around and saw the young employee of the gelateria running towards me. She was waving a receipt in her hand. It took me a moment until I realized that I had walked off without paying for my ice cream.

"I'm so sorry!" The whole piazza looked on while I fiddled through my bag in search of my purse. "I'm having a rough day. I swear I didn't mean to run off."

The young woman took the money. She didn't comment, but her scowl clearly said, "Yeah, that's what they all say."

I sat down on a bench and heard muted shouting again. This time from my phone.

"Oh, sorry, I didn't realize I started the call."

"What's going on?" Alexandra asked.

"I'm out of control."

"Problems at the border?"

"No, no, everything's fine on that front. Ida made it over with the help of a Swiss woman."

"Who is she?"

"A woman from Zurich. We met her on the train in Florence. I think she might be the reason why Ida wasn't taken off the train in Chiasso. Ida was sitting with Claudia and her children when the customs officers went through the train. She's been really lucky, and we thought..."

"What?"

"Do you think you could travel with her? She might need help on the way."

"Tonight?"

"She's got the ticket. I think it would be best if she could just keep going."

"I'm not sure... I'd have to check whether my daughter can stay over with friends tonight."

"Okay."

"Is it legal?"

"To travel with her?"

"Yes."

"I don't know."

"But do you think it is?"

"Probably not. But I guess in some situations all one can do is say, 'What the fuck?' and help. But I understand if you're worried. I'm not feeling like much of a hero myself right now." The mint and *fior di latte* ice cream was melting and running down my fingers to prove the point.

"Let me make a few phone calls. I'll get back to you in half an hour at the most."

"Okay."

I ended the call and observed the two slow-moving gelato trails that dropped from my left wrist onto my trousers. I got up to throw the whole cone into a trash can and searched my bag for a tissue to clean my hand. A group of locals, made up of a few unkempt youngsters and two fragile-looking old men in their best attire walked across the square, talking loudly, while I rubbed water onto my trousers. They carried leaflets for the ANPI, National Association of Italian Partisans, and were probably heading to the Liberation Day march that was winding through the Oltrarno quarter. I watched them, wondering whether the old men might have fought in the Resistance during Nazi Germany's occupation of Florence. Since reading my first history book about the Second World War, I had asked myself the age-old question: What would I have done? Would I have been brave enough to join the opposition under a brutal and repressive regime? At least I had my answer now. Even if had managed to muster the courage, a furious stalwart partisan would have sent me straight back home right after my first hour in action. No better way to blow up a meticulously planned undercover mission than by assigning it to a fretful and erratic woman prone to bursting into tears and running off without paying.

A text message from Alexandra arrived at last: *All clear for operation WTF. Talked to friends and colleagues from our independent refugee aid organisation in Zurich. Train safest option for everybody involved and Saturday night might be good timing for border crossing in Basel. I'm wearing a green coat and will be waiting under the main meeting point at the station.*

I called Claudia to relay Alexandra's message. She was relieved and passed me Ida, who I expected to be more anxious now that she had seen how many people had been stopped at the border in Chiasso.

"Mum, are you okay?"

"*I'm* okay. But what about you?"

"Don't worry. Allah sent me Claudia. I'm sure He'll help me

228

with the last part of the journey too. And mum, thank you so much. I'll always be grateful for what Claudia and you are doing for me."

"Don't worry. It's the least we can do," I said, comforted that not all of Ida's praise went straight up to heaven.

I got my bearings, and with Operation WTF safely on its way, got on the bus back to Siena. I picked up my car and was already driving through the Val d'Orcia when I received two messages one after the other. I stopped the car and read Alexandra and Claudia's texts, both of which confirmed that they had met in Zurich and all was well so far. I sat behind the steering wheel and watched the sun disappear behind the Tuscan hills. I was so tired that I couldn't even be bothered to get out of the car for the spectacular display of colors. I called Raffaella instead, my friend who had prepared the jollof rice for the girls in December. She lived nearby, and I was in need of a pick-me-up before facing the rest of the drive.

"What happened?" Raffaella asked, as soon as I walked into her kitchen. "You look terrible!"

"It's a long story."

"You need a pálinka."

Raffaella reached for a transparent bottle on top of a cupboard, poured me a bit into a small glass and explained that a Hungarian friend of hers recommended resorting to this high-percentage fruit brandy when everything else had failed. I had never heard of it, but after two sips from the tiny glass, a warm wave passed through my body and brought me back to life.

"Better?"

"A bit, yes." I told Raffaella about Ida, her horrendous trip to Europe and the cousin who was waiting for her in southern Germany.

"And where is she now?" Raffaella asked, after I had finished my account of the day.

"On the train from Zurich with a friend of mine." I checked my watch. "They'll be at the German border in Basel in less than half an hour."

"What will happen if the border guards stop them?"

"I don't think they could send Ida back to Italy. Her fingerprints haven't been taken yet. But she wouldn't be allowed to continue to Germany. She'd have to request asylum in Switzerland, which wouldn't help. She'd be less than two hours from her cousin but just as far away from her as she was in Italy. Neither of them would be allowed to cross the border to visit the other in Switzerland or Germany."

A call from Alexandra interrupted my explanation. It turned out that the border wasn't the only thing we had to worry about. The ticket I had bought for Ida had turned into a problem on the train from Zurich. Because it was ordered on the Internet, the printout of the ticket was valid only if it was handed to the conductor with proof of identification. This hadn't been necessary in Italy, where the numbered code was all Ida needed to show on the high-speed train, but in Switzerland, rules were rules and the conductor insisted on seeing Ida's passport. I should have known my home country better.

"What are you doing now?"

"I bought a new ticket for her on the train. After that, the conductor stopped nagging. But he could only sell us a ticket up to the border. He said we'll have to get a new one from the German conductor once we're on the other side. I hope that won't create any problems with the border guards when we cross over."

"Couldn't you—"

230

"We're getting close. I'll be in touch."

Alexandra hung up. Raffella looked at me.

"One more pálinka?"

"Better not. My stomach is in a knot, and I'm so tense I think I'll fall off the chair if I keep drinking... I just hope they make it."

"Shall I make tea?"

"No, thanks."

We sat there silently, waiting for news while I kept checking my watch. I had not once in my life crossed a border without a valid passport in hand and could only admire Ida for her resolution and her strength. I wished I had something to do. At least believers can kneel down and pray in moments like these.

Raffaella got up and walked to the other side of the room and turned on the stereo.

"I think this might help."

A familiar rhythm filled the long Tuscan living room, which had once been a shelter for cows and sheep. Patti Smith's voice followed a few beats later. The last time I heard "People Have the Power," the full moon was shining, and Patti and her band played the legendary tune for a madly dancing crowd on Siena's Piazza del Campo. Halfway through the song, Raffaella's husband came downstairs to see what was going on and enthusiastically joined our private restaging of that summer night.

"Repeat?" Raffaella asked, panting at the end of the song.

"Yes. No! Wait!"

I got my smartphone from the table, attached it to the stereo and scrolled through my Fela Kuti playlist. As an atheist, I couldn't implore Buddha, Allah, God Almighty or any other deity up in the sky. But I could put Fela's "Roforofo Fight" on and stomp my feet in the hope that somewhere along a border farther north, somebody would pick up the vibe.

We kept dancing the house down to my Fela playlist until the stereo amplified a whistle from my phone. Marco turned down the volume and handed me the phone. I read Alexandra's text once to myself, and then looked up to translate it for my sweating friends.

"Deutschland! On our way to Karlsruhe. No controls at the border. Long live Germany!" And a second message arrived right after: "German conductor on the train very friendly. Printout ticket fine with him and didn't bother to ask for Ida's ID. Wished us a safe journey and good luck instead!"

We looked at each other. The Germans! Like most Swiss, I had complained about them my whole life, and Italians were usually not their biggest fans either. But here they were, the good guys at last, nothing like the anal and narrow-minded train conductor of my home country. The Germans had managed to surprise us and would continue to do so for the rest of the year, while an ever-growing stream of people struggled along the Balkan route to knock on their door.

**

A third message arrived from Alexandra when I was on my way home: *On the train again. And thinking... crazy how the world can change.*

I had thought about that too.

Relatives of Alexandra's Jewish grandparents had tried to cross the exact same border in the opposite direction seventy-five years before. Turned away by the Swiss border guards, they died in the Holocaust.

21

The first thing I noticed back at the house was my pashmina. It lay neatly folded in the room on the ground floor that Ida had slept in, next to the old lady shoes and a fluorescent eighties sweater she had been given in Sicily. Ida had used the pashmina several times a day to cover her head during prayer. I unfolded it, wondering whether she hadn't taken it along because she didn't like it or because she had sensed that I hadn't dared to ask her to give it back. It was easy to donate suitcases, old dresses and pajamas, but I would have missed the Indian shawl—not the precious fabric in itself but all the stories that had been woven into it since a friend had given it to me for the birth of our daughter. But being so attached to a piece of embroidered cloth had felt downright embarrassing next to somebody who had lost her dearest people at sea.

I called Ida to ask how she was doing.

"I'm feeling a little bit better, mum. Having my cousin nearby helps."

"That's good!"

"And how are you?"

"Fine. I'm at work, I'll call again soon."

"Thank you! And mum..."

"What?"

Ida laughed. "See, Allah looked after me."

I had to laugh too. "Okay, I got it. You scored!"

Ida would need her faith, and all the courage she could muster, to build a new life for herself. But for my part—I wasn't going to turn into a believer just because some moody and unpredictable deity had at last decided to show up and pull some strings.

I put the pashmina into my bag and went upstairs to the kitchen. The Italian family had moved out, Vera was in her room and the girls were at Italian class. They participated in a free course the local municipalities offered to all the foreigners in the area. The lessons took place in the small village school, where the teacher had organized a separate class for the girls staying at the refugee home. I was happy to have a morning on my own to do some paper work and have a coffee and a chat with Vera. Lesley's mum had tried to support me, but not even the authority of an Igbo grandmother had managed to convince the girls to do more cleaning. The ambience at the house had gone from bad to worse since Joyce and the Italian family had moved out. After nine months, the girls were tired of waiting for their appointment with the commission in Florence and wanted to get out of the house. But where to? Rita spent most of her time in the city but insisted she couldn't stay with her friends when I suggested she live with them for good. Hope had become moody and didn't want to talk to me. Her work experience in the bar in Pisa had had the opposite effect than what I had hoped for, and she no longer showed any initiative after her first job trial hadn't worked out. Perhaps she was bothered by something else that had happened while she was away, but as always, I didn't really know.

I inspected the dirty stove and wondered whether to risk making a coffee, when Precious walked into the kitchen.

"Hi there, what are you doing here?" I said.

"Breakfast."

"I can see that. But you're late for class."

Precious didn't answer, looked for a clean cup and, since she couldn't find one, rinsed the least greasy one from the stack in the sink.

"Why aren't you at school?"

"I'm not going."

"Why? Are you feeling ill?"

"No."

"No? What's going on then?"

My phone rang, and I found out directly from the Italian teacher what was going on. None of the girls had shown up for the lesson, and the teacher didn't want to spend the whole hour waiting for them if they wouldn't arrive again.

"Again?" I asked.

"Same as last time. And the lesson before that, they arrived half an hour late and only Izogie came on time. She is the only one trying, even though it's more difficult for her than for most of the other girls."

"Where were the other girls?"

"I have no idea. But I don't think this makes any sense."

"Me neither!'

I ran up the stairs, taking two steps at a time, pulled open the bedroom doors on the second floor and yelled like a drill sergeant ordering his misbehaving recruits to get back in line. Hope, Precious, Fola and Izogie crawled out of their beds but had no aspiration whatsoever to resemble a platoon of soldiers. Following the adage that the best defense is a good offense, they drowned my order to get up and run to school in an assault of shouting. The classes were no good. The teacher was no good. And I was no good at organizing a proper Italian lesson for them in the first place.

I shouted back for a while (the classes were good, the teacher did her best and it was impossible to teach them anything if they behaved like this), but I should have known better. It was an ironclad rule of operators working in refugee homes to avoid any kind of debate with groups consisting of more than one Nigerian. And this was advice put forward by Italians, people like Maria, who definitely had the vigorous genetic makeup to sustain a shouting match or two.

"Holy shit, girls—"

"Mum, don't talk to us in bad language!" Hope shouted.

"I'll use bad language until you stop shouting at me."

Fola jumped back into bed and pulled the blanket over her head. The other girls kept yelling that I couldn't boss them around. I went downstairs, tried to calm down and called Maria for advice. She told me what I already knew.

"Don't discuss anything with them in a group. And tell them that the new organization won't accept this kind of behavior. I'll come up next week with Domenico to give you support with this."

"I'm sorry, but this can't wait 'til next week. I have tried to help where I could. They either start playing by the rules or they need to move somewhere else."

"That kind of thing needs to be discussed with the prefecture first."

"I know. Can you send me an example of a letter of complaint from your refugee home?"

"Sure."

I went upstairs and gave them an ultimatum.

"I'm going to inform the prefecture, unless you go to school right now. I'll call the teacher to let her—"

"We're not going!" Hope said, to the clapping of the other girls.

"And you'll also have to clean the kitchen the way you used to with Lesley as soon as you're back from school."

"We're not taking any orders from you." Fola had come out from under the blanket to paint her nails.

"This is not an order, it's your responsibility. You signed a contract when you moved in here, and if you want to live here, you have to respect your side of it."

"We'll tell the police and the people from the new organization that you treat us badly!" Fola shouted, while waving her electric-blue nails through the air.

"I'm not cleaning anything," Izogie said. "It was Precious's turn."

"Okay, Precious, you'll clean the kitchen when you get back from school."

"I won't." Precious crossed her arms in front of her chest and looked at me defiantly.

"She never cleans, so I don't see why we should," Hope said, while crossing her arms like Precious.

"I'm not going to discuss this as a group. Each of you come down to the office, and we'll talk it through one-on-one. Who's coming down first?"

Nobody answered.

"Look. We can't continue like this. You either start to cooperate, or I'll send that letter to the prefecture. Who's coming down to talk to me?"

"We're not talking to you," Fola said, and Hope added, "We'll only talk to the staff of the new organization. They are much more professional than you."

"I'm sure they are, but until they're here you're going to have to make do with me."

"We won't!" all four of them said in unison.

"I think it's about time you remembered that I'm the person who helped each time one of you was in a tight spot."

"Nobody said you had to help!" Hope said, to the nodding of the other girls.

"But I did, even though I haven't even been paid yet for the work I'm doing here."

"It's not our fault if you and Lesley aren't paid. You could have left!" Precious said.

"Okay, forget it. Who's coming down with me?"

Nobody answered.

"Hope?"

Hope turned her lips into a pout, lifted her head and looked away from me.

"Izogie?"

Izogie clicked her tongue.

"Fola?"

"Are you through?" Precious said before I could finish my round.

Was I? The four girls I had spent so much time with in the past nine months looked at me with apparent disdain. A half-eaten plate of jollof rice was balanced precariously on a bedside table. A heap of dirty sheets Precious was supposed to wash lay in exactly the same spot as the week before.

"Yes, I'm through."

I went downstairs to get my bag and drove home to type the letters of complaint. One for each girl. I mentioned their refusal to participate in the Italian lessons, the dismal state of the house and their often disrespectful behavior towards me, Lesley and Vera. I wrote a separate letter for Rita. She was traveling and normally did her share of cleaning in the house, but she hardly ever joined the literacy and Italian classes, and kept inventing new excuses why she couldn't. I read over the letters and felt like a petty informer, an Italian version of the Stasi spy. There had to be a better way. I called Lesley and told her what was happening.

"These girls wouldn't get away with any of this in Nigeria," Lesley said after listening to me. "Send it off! I don't have a clue what's going on in their heads. But don't think this is acceptable behavior where I come from."

I sent the email with the attached letters to the prefecture and printed a copy for each of the girls. Then I went back to the house to translate the letters for them in the afternoon. They weren't around. I decided to stay in Dogana to wait for them. They got back in the early evening on the last bus from the city. They were dressed in their best wigs and clothes and looked like a Nigerian girl group back from a concert in Rome. I handed out the letters and explained that they would be expelled from the project if they kept behaving like this. One more of these letters and they would have to leave. Hope, Precious and Fola walked off without saying anything. Izogie was the only one who wanted to know what was written in the letter. I translated it for her. She nodded her head, and said she was sorry and that she'd go back to the lessons.

I stopped at the bar in Dogana, ordered a Campari and wrote an email to the new team.

Dear Pio, Domenico and Maria

my contract finished today. I'd like to continue our collaboration, but I have some serious doubts about the value of the work I'm doing here. In the past year, Lesley and I have tried to establish a relationship of trust and create a warm and family-like ambience in the house. Assuming that most girls have been trafficked to Italy, our objective was to offer support, prevention and a way out. One of the girls (Izogie) has learned to read and write in her time here, and Joyce has managed to find a job as a babysitter in Rome (this, at least, is what we're being told). But looking at the human and economic resources that are being invested into this project, and comparing them with the few "results" we have achieved, I seriously doubt that standard refugee shelters are the right places for the many girls arriving from Nigeria.

For the last twenty years, young women from Nigeria have made up an ever-growing percentage of the sex workers on Italy's and Europe's roads. It is well known that most of the girls arrive via the Mediterranean route, after having been held under horrendous circumstances in brothels and ghettos in Libya. Nevertheless, in my time working here, I haven't found a program that directly addresses these issues once the Nigerian women arrive in Italy, or once they are sent to the country's refugee shelters. Considering their particular situation, I don't think it makes sense to just follow through with the standard protocol for asylum seekers. My approach might have been wrong (and the precarious state of the organization Lesley and I worked for surely didn't help), but the situation doesn't seem any different in Tuscan refugee homes that are more stable and better structured than ours. Instead of presenting an obstacle that can interrupt the vicious cycle of human trafficking, the shelters seem to have become ideal repositories for the traffickers and madams: the girls can be called for days of work on the road before they are sent back to the refugee homes, which take care of the paper work, legal procedures, health problems or interruptions of pregnancies while the government pays for room and board.

These are extremely complex situations, and I am aware that there are no shortcuts to resolving them. But since our approach is not leading anywhere, I can't see the point in continuing along the same modalities. Let's meet to discuss all of this and also to figure out what to do about my contract, which expired today, April 30.

Best,
Katja

I sent the email from the bar, ordered a second Campari and leafed through an old newspaper somebody had left on the counter. I browsed through the usual mix of news about Italy's economic crisis and various scandals involving the country's politicians, skipped the pages with the results of the local soccer teams and stopped to read an article about the murder of a Nigerian woman in a pinewood near Pisa. Forty-six-year-old Iriagbonse Eghianruwa was born in Benin City. She was stabbed to death on the last day of March, and two German tourists found her body close to a roadside stop. Operators of a charity supporting sex workers in Pisa told the press that Iriagbonse's son was about to graduate from medical school in Nigeria. Her children had been able to study thanks to the money she kept sending home.

I swirled the blood-red Campari in front of me. It had entirely lost its appeal. I pushed the glass to the other side of the table and thought of Chika Unigwe's *On Black Sisters' Street*, a fine and painstakingly researched novel that I had read a couple of months before. Unigwe tells the story of four Nigerian women who work as prostitutes in Belgium. Two of the young women use their earnings as a launching pad for a better life back in Nigeria. One stays in Belgium and becomes a madam herself. The fourth is murdered, not by a client, as Iriagbonse was in the pinewood near Pisa, but by the people who had trafficked her to Europe when the young woman attempts to run off before paying her "debt."

***

Izogie called me two days later. It was eleven o'clock on Saturday night.

"Fola and Hope are fighting. We need help."

I heard screaming in the background. A lot of it. I hung up to call Dante. The police officer had left me his cell phone number after Izogie and Rita had fought with each other exactly a month ago. He was on duty and called me from the house half an hour later.

"We need you to come up. Both girls are hurt. The doctor is arriving, and we need somebody to translate in case they have to be taken to the hospital."

I had been sitting in the kitchen, waiting for news and already dressed. Sergio came to the door and shook his head.

"You're going up?"

"Obviously."

"I just wanted to remind you that you're working again without a contract."

"I know. I'm going to figure it out with them next week. I've definitely had enough of this. But I can't let Dante down right now. He helped last time too."

"So you keep working on a weekend, even though you still

haven't been paid."

"Pio promised I would be paid for April in the second half of May. I'm just going to have to take his word for it."

"*Parole, parole, parole,*" Sergio sang while I got out the door. Words, words, words.

The situation was still tense when I arrived in Dogana. Two police officers were sitting with Fola in the kitchen. Vera, Precious, Rita and Dante were in the living room, standing around Hope while the local doctor inspected her lower lip.

"Looks like a bite wound," he said. "She has to be taken to the hospital. She'll need stitches."

"What about Fola?" I asked.

"The other girl? I already looked at her. She has a swollen eye and says she had to throw up after the fight. She might have a concussion. I'd rather she got checked too."

"You can't have them travel in the same ambulance," Dante intervened. "The girl in the kitchen hasn't calmed down yet."

We discussed the options. The local ambulance had just taken somebody to the hospital and needed at least half an hour to get to Dogana. The doctor offered to drive Hope and me in his car, even though he wasn't allowed to do so, as the vehicle was the property of the national health service. I was startled for a moment by the absurdity of a doctor not being allowed to transport patients and—knowing that Italians could be very law-abiding when I least expected it—thanked the doctor for making an exception. He drove to the hospital with Hope and me while the carabinieri waited with Fola for the ambulance.

Dante had told me it seemed like the fight might have started because Hope had offended Fola's family. I wondered which family. Fola had grown up on the streets of Benin City and was at times taken in by improvised foster parents, but never for long. Fola had told us that she had never met her father and she couldn't remember her mother. She only knew that she had been called Fola, a popular Yoruba name, because her mother had moved to Benin City from Yorubaland.

I tried to ask Hope some questions about what happened, but she couldn't talk with her split lip, and I doubted she would have wanted to talk to me even if she could.

The nurse at the emergency ward called a young doctor, who shook his head when he saw Hope's wound.

"Such a beautiful lip. What a shame!" He turned around and asked the nurse to prepare a syringe for a local anesthetic. "I'll try my best to stitch this up nicely."

I could hardly watch the procedure but was relieved that the doctor set to work without saying anything more. The last thing I needed was a moralizing tirade in the emergency ward at two in the morning.

I stood next to Hope, who was wincing with pain, and thought of the quarantine room we had been sitting in on that long August day nine months before. So much had happened in the meantime, but unlike what I had expected then, nothing had changed for the better.

Fola arrived with the ambulance as Hope's lip was being stitched back together. A doctor ran some tests and confirmed that everything was fine with her. We could take the girls home. I asked whether one of them could stay for the night, but the staff insisted that there was no need. I talked to the doctor who had brought us in about how to get back to the house. I wasn't looking forward to sitting in the same car with Hope and Fola, but they were both exhausted, and so were we. We left the hospital and got into the car: Hope in the front with the doctor and me in the back with Fola, who luckily fell asleep as soon as she touched the seat. She didn't even wake up when the doctor had to hit the brakes to dodge a deer crossing the road. He slowed down again a bit farther on because of two porcupines that scurried along the lane.

"What a crazy night," I said, dead tired and totally disillusioned.

"Oh, this is nothing," the doctor answered. "With a moon like this, I sometimes have to stop several times each mile: wild boars, deer, porcupines, badgers... you wouldn't believe what's going on here at night."

The doctor dropped us off, and I accompanied the girls inside and instructed them to stay out of each other's way. Ground floor only for Fola, and second floor only for Hope. I had no idea whether it would work, but at four in the morning, all I wanted was to get back home to go to bed.

I drove off and screeched to a halt shortly after Dogana. A doe, followed by two fawns. They ran through the triangle illuminated by the car's headlights, before I watched them disappear—one after the other—back into the dark undergrowth that lay right next to the road.

22

I stood on the terrace of the refugee home and observed Dogana's village life.

Two old men walked past.

A stray cat slept on a bench.

The mumbled sound of a daytime talk show made its way across the piazza. After awhile, somebody coughed and turned it off.

Surely, Hope wasn't going to miss Tuscany's slow-paced countryside life. Other things maybe, but not this. She and Fola would be expelled from the refugee home. The prefecture hadn't received the exact date yet, but the vice-prefect had let me know that we could expect a call from the immigration office soon.

A car arrived and parked. Pio, Domenico and Maria got out of it, and I went indoors to put on the coffee. After receiving my email, Maria had proposed a meeting in the city during the week, but after what happened on Saturday night, the team had agreed to make time to come up to the house first thing on Monday morning.

I had placed a table and a few chairs in the shade of the terrace. We sat down, and after pouring the coffee, I started with a short update about Saturday night and my communications with the prefecture.

Pio nodded and thanked me for handling everything. "Calling

the carabinieri was the right thing to do." He turned to Domenico. "Do you want to carry on from here?"

"Sure," Domenico said, looking at a handwritten list in front of him. "Let's go through the urgent things first. Your communications with the prefecture..."

"Yes?"

"We noticed that you are very precise with the reporting of the daily presence list."

"Sure," I said. I looked around the table and realized that it hadn't been meant as a compliment. "Why, what's wrong with that?"

"There is nothing wrong with that, but considering the financial situation..." Domenico left the end of the sentence open for interpretation.

"Let's say you don't have to be quite as Swiss about it," Pio said, beaming at me in his friendly manner.

"About what?"

"The exact number on the presence list," Domenico said. "We normally notify the prefecture of the absence of a refugee only the day after he or she has actually left to travel. This gives us an extra day that is covered financially. After all, on the day the refugees leave they often still have breakfast or even lunch at the house, and we have to pay for that. Hence, it's only right that these costs are being taken into account and covered by the government."

I looked around the table. I had wanted to discuss the workings of Nigerian prostitution rings and how to better manage the situation with the young women in the house, but my new bosses' priorities evidently lay somewhere else.

"Don't worry too much about it." Maria must have noticed my perplexed expression. "You only have to keep notifying the prefecture for the next month or so. We're planning to organize things differently, and from summer on, we'll combine the presence lists of all refugee homes at our office. That way, the shelters won't have to communicate directly with the prefecture. You'll send the daily presence report to Domenico, and he will update the list of all the homes before sending it on to the vice-prefect. This will simplify things for everybody involved."

And it will also provide the time for your organization to fiddle around a bit with the numbers, I thought. But instead I said, "I hoped we'd be talking about the email I sent you last week."

"Absolutely." Maria took a sip of her coffee. "We have discussed the situation on the way up here, and we realized where the problem lies. You need more support, and Lesley is never around to help you."

Their take on the matter kept surprising me. "I agree that I need more support. And I definitely don't plan to keep spending my Saturday nights like this. But Lesley isn't around at the moment because she doesn't have a contract."

"Sure, but she lives here for free," Maria said, placing her espresso cup carefully back on the saucer.

"With her mother," Domenico added.

"So you think this is the type of work people should be doing in exchange for a free bed?"

"That's not what we were trying to say, but you have to understand—"

"Lesley has been sent here because of a crazy but influential Italian husband who is still threatening to kill her. She was supposed to find protection and support in this house, but everybody seems busy finding a way to get rid of her instead of helping her get her children back!"

"We are sorry about that, but sadly, with the financial situation

Teresa left behind, there is nothing we can do to help."

"Yes, you can. You can hire her. As you say, this home is going to need more staff, and Lesley needs a job. And one that's actually being paid. It's as easy as that. She has been working here since last summer. She has fulfilled her part of the deal, but Teresa's organization hasn't!"

"We don't think it was a good deal," Maria said.

"Me neither! For none of us!"

Pio cleared his voice. "I can assure you that we don't take this situation lightly, but our first aim has to be the financial stability of the organization. We need to make sure we'll be able to help people in the future. We canceled several important meetings to make sure we could come to Dogana this morning. But before we start discussing your contract, I need to know one thing from you..." Pio paused to make sure he had everybody's attention. "How are you?"

"Me?" I thought of Ida's answer to that question. "A little bit well" is what she always said. "Not great right now."

"That's what I thought. We can fully understand that. We're still happy to offer you this job, but we obviously need to know whether you are really up for it."

"I'm still interested in the content of this work but not in this form. I don't think what we're doing here is working."

"Yes," Pio nodded, "you wrote that in your email."

"And I can't see the point in doing something we know doesn't work. Even more so if the approach costs the Italian taxpayer a lot of money but doesn't resolve anything."

"I can understand that you're disillusioned. I have worked with drug addicts for years, and sadly, that's just how it is." Pio leaned back in his chair, sighed and folded his arms on top of his head. Maria and Domenico nodded in agreement. It seemed

249

I was the only one who couldn't see the connection.

"No, sorry, I don't get it. These girls may be a handful, and they are no doubt in a difficult situation, but they are definitely not drug addicts!"

"I understand that. But I can tell you from my long-standing experience that this is just the reality of social work. Things need time. You can't expect people to change overnight."

"I don't expect people to change overnight. But after nine months of doing this, I can't see why we should continue with an approach if it doesn't work."

"Yes, you said so. But what do you want to do about the job?"

I didn't have a clue. I was tired and at the same time still wanted to find a better way. I had seen too much of Italy's underbelly to just pretend nothing had happened. Europe's enlightenment had evidently stopped way before shining the spotlight on the sexual needs and practices of the continents' inhabitants. The oldest profession in the world was, absurdly, still the only one with zero workers' rights. But why talk about our society's taboos and risk waking a sleeping giant as long as the job was done just fine by foreign girls who could always be substituted with new ones?

"I think I need a break to think about it."

"Sure," Pio said, while putting the cups back on the tray. "Put your feet up for a couple of days. We'll manage things here. No phone calls, no nothing from our side. Let me know latest by Thursday morning what you have decided to do."

***

I had a backlog of all my other work and used my time-out from the refugee home to get back on top of things. On Tuesday, I did some research for an article about good restaurants on the

Tuscan coast and, after a long walk with our dog, topped up my Instagram and Facebook feeds with photos of a couple of cypress trees and a gorgeous sunset. It made for a lovely life—why had I ever wanted to meddle in anything else?

On Wednesday, I drove to the city. My laptop needed an overhaul and I was standing in the lineup in the computer shop when Maria called. I had talked with a couple of friends and hadn't decided yet what to do about the job, but Maria's phone call was about to change that.

"Sorry to bother you today, but we've got a new arrival for the house in Dogana and I need to know whether the rooms are ready."

"Yes, they are. We've got three rooms, two double and one single. I just need to tell the girls or Lesley's mum to put fresh sheets on the beds. Who is arriving?"

"Three women from Syria. A mother traveling with her two grown-up daughters. One of them is physically and mentally disabled and will need special medical care. I am with them at the emergency reception center right now."

"When will you take them to Dogana?"

"Today. We need to free up the reception center for new arrivals. I just have to organize the transport. A volunteer is free this afternoon, but we won't all fit into his car. Amira will come along to translate."

"I'm here in the city. I can help."

I called Izogie and Vera and asked them to prepare the beds for our new guests before I drove to the reception center to pick up Maria. Nour and her daughters, Farah and Leila, were already in the car with the volunteer and Amira, the cultural meditator for the emergency reception center, who was originally from Egypt. In Dogana, I showed them the house while Amira translated.

It turned out that Farah spoke good English, and once Amira and Maria had left, she started translating for her mother, who wanted to tell me that the view from the house reminded her of the valleys near Damascus.

"This is a compliment," Farah added. "My mother loves those valleys." Nour also asked Farah to translate that she and her daughters were very grateful to be able to stay in such a beautiful place. In turn, I asked Farah to tell her mother that we were very happy to have them staying in Dogana.

Nour ran a bath for Leila, who needed continuous support. In the meantime, I explained to Farah how to work the stove in the kitchen and asked how they had managed to care for Leila on the trip.

"It was difficult," Farah said, while turning the stove on and off. "The flight from Turkey to Libya was the easy bit. But Tripoli and the boat ride to Sicily... We were dropped at a beach and told to walk towards the boat. We walked in until we were up to our chest in the water, trying to hold up Leila between us. My mother just kept praying and praying."

Later in the day, Nour would dry pages of the Koran on the balcony of the refugee home. The holy book had traveled on her chest and had been soaked through in Mediterranean water.

"Could I send a message from your phone?" Farah asked. "We need to get in touch with my brother. I have a phone but no SIM card."

"Sure! Where is he?"

"In Berlin."

Farah sent a WhatsApp message to her brother. He called back immediately. Standing next to Farah, I could hear his excitement through the phone, even though they spoke in Arabic. The last news he had had from his mother and sisters was from

Istanbul, before they boarded the plane to Tripoli. Nour and her daughters had been among the last Syrians to take this route before Turkey shut down flights to Libya and more and more people started to travel the Balkan route.

Farah handed me the phone and asked me to talk to her brother. Sayid wanted to know where exactly his family was staying in Italy and whether I could indicate the closest airport and public transport that would take him to the refugee home. He wanted to book a flight to Italy quickly, so as to accompany and support his mother and sisters during their trip to Germany. They would have to cross two European borders illegally to get there from Italy.

"Are you sure? We are very happy to have them here with us. Leila is getting her medications, and we'll also make sure she gets a checkup with a specialist."

"My mother's dream is to have us all back together as a family. I'm sorry to ask you for help with this, but I hope you'll understand. My mother hasn't seen my children for over three years."

Of course I understood, but at the same time, I didn't want to let them go. Nour and her daughters had escaped from a war-torn country and would certainly be granted asylum in Italy. They brought along their own traumas, but I also knew that with them, my daily routine at the house wouldn't consist of researching prostitution and dealing with the opaque machinations of criminal organizations.

I called Pio to explain the situation and asked whether Sayid could stay at the house for a night before he traveled up north with his family. He said he didn't think it was a problem, but he'd rather I'd talked with Maria about it. I called Maria, who said she was very sorry, but their organization had a clear government contract for the running of refugee homes; hence, we had to respect the procedure and couldn't let Nour's son stay the night. I reminded her that we had enough free beds and it would be for one night only. She reminded me that we had very strict guidelines from the prefecture and she wasn't going to mess with them. The refugee home in Dogana wasn't a hotel, after all.

I called Sergio, who started cursing the moment I told him that I was back in Dogana and needed help.

"*Porco dio*, what the hell is it now?"

I told him to calm down and explained about Nour and her family and that Sayid needed a bed for a night.

"Yes, obviously, he can stay at our place. You could have told me right away. I thought you were stuck in some emergency ward again."

***

Sayid arrived in Italy two days later. He had been granted refugee status in Germany and had been able to book a flight from Berlin to Pisa thanks to his permit of stay and Syrian passport. From Pisa, he continued his journey by train. Amira was supposed to pick him up at the station in the city and help him get on the right bus to Dogana. But they waited in vain. I called Sergio, who was already close to the city to do the weekly food shopping for our family. He drove to the station from the supermarket and dropped Sayid in Dogana at 9 PM.

The family hugged each other, and Leila was so excited, she didn't want to let go of her brother. They sat on the sofa together while we discussed the travel options by train. We talked to Amira again to see whether she had any updated information. A lot of the Syrians arriving at the reception center moved on as soon as possible and sometimes let her know whether and where they had made it over the border. Sayid decided to travel via Milan in the end, as he had heard that they might be able to find help and advice there from members of northern Italy's Syrian community.

I felt sorry that I had to take them to the train station the next morning. Nour and her daughters had been at the house for only a few days, but I knew that I would miss her family and the fact that it had been so easy to get along with the three of them. Syria's culture and the belief system of Islam weren't any closer to mine than the ones of the Christian girls from Nigeria, but the difference was that Nour's family had been part of the middle class and this created a common ground that exceeded nationality and religion. Class and education turned out to be bigger dividers than race and religious beliefs. Had Joyce, Hope, Precious, Fola, Izogie and Rita had the educational options and middle-class upbringing of Nour's children or myself, their life path wouldn't have brought them to a Tuscan refugee home and sex work on an Italian road.

At twenty-three, Farah had a degree in information science, and her mother had worked her whole life in public administration. She had retired shortly before the war and had paid for her family's trip to Europe with her life savings. Unlike her daughters, Nour still wore a headscarf in public and traveled with the Koran, but she had an independence and autonomy that didn't seem much different from my own mother's, who had also raised her children on her own and as the only breadwinner in the family. But even though the special care Leila needed could have been organized in Tuscany too, I also knew that Farah's professional future would look much more promising in a city like Berlin than a Tuscan hilltop town.

It was getting late, and I felt embarrassed interrupting the long-awaited family reunion to tell Sayid that he would have to sleep at our place. Vera and Izogie had been sitting with us in the living room, and both intervened to say that they were happy to help prepare a bed, and Sayid insisted that he could easily spend the night on the sofa. Leila hugged her brother even tighter, and I remembered the conversation I had had with Pio and his team at the beginning of the week. If they didn't have a problem with adjusting the numbers of their shelters' refugee presence lists to get a few extra euros from the government, they better get used to disregarding the guidelines when it came to helping a family in need.

"Okay then, Vera and Izogie will prepare a bed for you," I told Sayid. "I'll be back at nine. Make sure you're ready."

"We will! And thank you. We really appreciate it."

"No problem. But Sayid, please don't smoke in the house. You can use the balcony."

"Sure. My mum already told me to smoke out there. She says the hills and the olive groves look just like the place we always went to for our Sunday outings from Damascus."

***

The following morning, I picked up Nour and her children to drive them to the city. It was a Saturday, and Amira planned to meet us at the train station, since she didn't have to work. She wanted to say good-bye and make sure the family had all the information they needed for the trip.

Sayid was sitting up front, telling me that he liked our car and that he had enjoyed the ride to Dogana with Sergio. "You have a very nice man. We talked about a lot of things last night: raising children, the war, soccer..."

"You did? How?" I looked over at Sayid. "Sergio hardly speaks any English."

"Oh no, he speaks the language very well!"

Men, I thought.

Sayid pulled out a pack of chewing gums, offered a piece to everybody in the car and then rolled down the window to throw out a wrapper.

"Stop!" I yelled.

"What?"

"You can't just throw it out the window. You're in a car with a Swiss. We're ruthless when it comes to littering."

Sayid laughed and said something in Arabic to his family, until they all joined in.

"What's so funny?" I asked.

"I just thought of my mum! Back home, when she emptied a can of tomato sauce, she'd just throw it out the window into the courtyard."

"You're kidding?"

"No, no, it's true," Sayid said, still laughing. "We kids had to collect them, but we always had to be careful not do it when she was just opening another."

I imagined their home in Damascus, with a younger version of Nour standing in the kitchen, and her children and late husband carefully ducking through the courtyard each time their mother and wife was about to prepare a meal.

"Hit by a tomato can!" Now I had to laugh. "So, is that how your father died?"

Sayid turned to look at me, and I cursed myself for blurting out something like that without thinking.

"Hit by a tomato can..." He chuckled and translated for his mother, who laughed so hard the whole car seemed to wobble.

When we reached the outskirts of the city, Nour pointed to a building from the seventies or eighties. Sayid told me that his mum thought it looked similar to the house they had lived in in Damascus.

"And this one," Farah said, translating for Nour and indicating a palazzo with a bleached facade, "this looks just like our mother's office."

Sayid stopped chatting and silently observed the passing scenery. After awhile, I asked him whether he too thought this area looked a bit like their neighborhood in Damascus. Sayid didn't say anything and kept staring out the window. I was parking the car in front of the station when he finally answered.

"I wish Damascus looked like this." He bent down to grab his bag and opened the car door, "but the city my mother remembers no longer exists."

23

The immigration officer got up to welcome us. Hope and Fola sat down on the brown office chairs in front of his desk, and I pulled up a plastic chair next to them. The officer walked back to his desk with a wide smile on his face. I wondered what was going on. This grumpy servant of the state had hardly looked up from his files the other times we'd been in his office.

"Would you translate for me?" he asked.

"Sure," I said, thinking of the first time I had helped with translating. Fola was feeling sick, and I had censored some of the more questionable things the officer had said to her. This time, I would translate everything, no matter what he came out with. After all, filtering out stupid comments was almost as patronizing as making them.

"Please tell the two young ladies, that I don't agree with the prefecture's decision to expel them from the project."

"You don't?" I couldn't believe my ears.

"Not at all. Sadly, the final decision isn't up to me, but if it was, I certainly wouldn't send them away. They'll end up on the road like this!"

Only a few months had passed since the officer had tried to impede Fola and Precious's return to Dogana after they had spent some time on said road. Then he had tried to boycott the vice-prefect's decision to let them back into the project. I was surprised to see him side with the girls now. Evidently, whatever the prefect or vice-prefect decided, the officer made sure he'd support the exact opposite. It was the revolt of the frustrated bureaucrat. That his petty internal warfare put people's lives on hold out in the real world didn't seem to bother him.

Fola and Hope signed the documents that listed their fight and recurring disrespectful behavior as the reasons why they were expelled from the refugee home. They didn't say a word, but Fola's eyes filled with tears when we left the office. It was the second time that I had seen her cry, but I also knew this wasn't the first time in her life that she had ended up on the road. Fola would get by. Somehow. She was streetwise and, under her bubbly exterior, tougher than most. In the car, Fola dried her tears, made a phone call and, a couple of minutes later, was already laughing. Not dwelling on things gone wrong was probably one of the first things one had to learn when growing up on the road.

I drove the girls to the charity's office in the city, where they picked up their remaining pocket money. It was enough for a train ticket into a new life, not much more. From there we continued to the train station. Fola and I got out of the car and I accompanied her to the ticket machine where I had picked her up only a few months before. Hope waited in the car. The two of them still didn't talk.

Fola bought a ticket to Rome and we said goodbye.

"And Fola—" I said before she turned to go.

"Mum?"

"Next time somebody gives you a second chance, make sure you make the best of it." My words sounded hollow and preachy even to me. Fola was standing at a train station with twenty euros in her pocket and a suitcase filled with skimpy clothes. There was no need to rub it in.

I watched Fola disappear among the travelers and wondered whether I'd ever see her again. Ten days had passed since I had dropped Nour and her children at the same station. Sayid had texted me from Milan, where his mother and sisters had spent a night sleeping on the benches in the station while he had tried to find information on how best to cross the border. Two days later, I received a WhatsApp message with a photo of the four of them waving from a train station in Germany. They looked tired, but happy.

After dropping off Fola, Hope and I drove to a clinic to book an appointment for the removal of the stitches in her lip.

"Do you want to get back to the station?" I asked.

"No, it's fine. You can leave me here."

"Have you found a place to stay?"

"I have to make some phone calls."

"What about your boyfriend in Pisa?"

"There is no boyfriend in Pisa." Hope pulled her suitcase out of the trunk. "What about my hearing with the commission?"

"The officer will let me know once he receives the dates from Florence. You'll have to go back to the immigration office to pick up the paper work stating the time and place of the appointment. They'll ask you to sign the papers to prove that you were notified in time."

By now, the girls had been waiting for their appointment with the commission in Florence for ten months.

"Fine. I'll let you know if I change my number."

"Okay. And let me know how you're getting on."

Hope nodded and walked off. I drove back to the charity's office to sign my contract. The arrival of Nour and her family had convinced me to keep working for the charity. However, the refugee home had to be organized differently for it to work properly. Pio and his team had initially planned to transfer five Nigerian women who were staying at the refugee home in the city to the one in Dogana. But they agreed that this wasn't a good idea after the fights that had happened in April and May. To become financially viable, the house in Dogana needed to be able to receive male refugees, since it was the young men arriving from Western Africa who were most likely to stay in Italy. With the warm season, the arrivals in Sicily were booming again. Pio handed me the contract to look through and explained that Domenico had already brought the matter to the attention of the prefecture. Running shelters for both genders was normal practice; Dogana had only followed different guidelines because of its initial setup as a women's shelter.

"And regarding your contract, you'll see it's valid until the end of the year. I decided to hire you all the way through to December!" Pio smiled at me as if he was giving me an unexpected promotion.

"Great," I said, wondering what the other option would have been. Preparing a new contract for me month to month? I read through the printout, which looked good, until I scanned the financial details. The contract started from mid-May, which meant that I would receive only half the salary for the current month.

"Sorry, but I can't sign this unless I'm paid for all of May."

Pio took the contract back and looked through the paragraph that mentioned my salary. "That must have been a misunderstanding between me and the administration." He called his secretary and told her about the needed changes. "We'll get the corrected version to you in a couple of days. You'll obviously be paid for all the work you've done for us."

"What about the outstanding wages?"

"Your April salary will arrive in your account in the second half of this month."

"And the other eight months?"

"We're still looking into that. Sadly, the debts of the old organization are so big that I can't promise anything right now."

***

Things were quiet at the refugee home for the rest of the month. Pio and Maria had asked me to turn the yoga room into an extra bedroom, and Aziz and his Gambian friends accompanied me to Dogana one day to help move the heavy rehabilitation machines—leftovers from the earlier days—that were taking up a lot of space. Once they were stacked against the wall, the lower floor had a new bedroom and started to look good. But the rest of the house kept falling apart. Precious kept skipping her cleaning turns, Izogie and Rita refused to pick up the slack, and I had no energy or patience left to discuss the house rules with any of them. I needed a new start with new people, and a proper contract and salary at last.

***

On the last weekend of May, Sergio had organized *La Scalata del Camparista*, a crazy bicycle race in the vicinity of our village. It was really just a pretext for a good party, and I hadn't the least intention of participating in Sergio's strangely heroic adventures. But I was looking forward to the after-race lunch in our village, which would be accompanied by a concert by Hotel Rif. The members of the folk band, which had been founded by a family friend, had traveled down from the Veneto region in the northeast for the big event. But instead of enjoying the concert, I spent the afternoon at the refugee home in Dogana. The electricity had stopped working and it took ages to find a technician who had time to come and look for the problem on a Sunday afternoon.

When I got back to our village, the piazza was deserted. People were having their coffee at the counter in the bar, and the musicians of Hotel Rif had just finished packing up their instruments. Sergio's team was still celebrating with countless rounds of Campari, but I had missed too much of the party to be able to catch up. I went home instead and checked my online bank account. The April salary wasn't in it, I still hadn't received the corrected contract from the charity and I had spent another Sunday sorting out emergencies at the refugee home instead of having a good time with my family and friends.

I called Maria the following day—June 1—to tell her that I wouldn't come back to Dogana unless I was paid immediately. She thought I was overreacting and asked me to be patient. Their charity always paid. Surely, this was something that could be sorted out. I lost my cool and shouted down the phone that I had no patience left. Not an inkling.

I tried to call Pio. The line was busy, and shortly after, a message arrived from Maria.

Spoke with Pio. Your April salary was paid ten days ago!!!

I read the message twice. I had been paid ten days ago? Was I losing it? I opened my laptop and checked my online bank account once more.

Nothing.

I tried to call Pio again. He didn't answer. I sent Pio and Maria a message saying that I had checked my bank account, that the money wasn't there and that I expected to hear from them. The next day, I sent Maria all the information she needed for running the refugee home in Dogana but didn't hear back from her or Pio about my salary. I called Rita, Izogie and Precious to let them know that I wouldn't be back. Precious seemed relieved. Rita and Izogie said they were sorry. Izogie promised she would keep reading.

On Wednesday, I was on my way to Pienza in the Val d'Orcia for a lunch date with the journalist I had wanted to meet since December. I was driving past Montalcino when my phone beeped. An email from Pio. It was about time! I pulled into a rest stop to open it.

Subject: Bank transfer

Attached is the copy of the bank transfer of your April wages, which was executed on May 19 and confirms—as we already told you several times—that you have been paid. Having been informed of the disrespectful tone of voice you used in the conversation with your superior Maria Doronzo, I am expecting your immediate resignation.

I'd also like to remind you of the utmost seriousness of our charity, which ALWAYS fulfills ALL the commitments undertaken with its employees.

Always available for a serene conversation in our office, I salute you respectfully,
Pio Sanelli

I reread the email, which made me feel like a first grader who had dared to criticize the principal. I opened the attachment, wondering where my money had gone. It was the copy of a bank transfer executed on May 19. It had my name on it and stated

"April salary," but the bank account number was definitely not mine. I called a friend who worked in a bank. She explained that the international bank account number indicated on the transfer was the only thing that counted.

I started the car and drove to Raffaella's. She was working in the garden and didn't look surprised when I pulled up in front of her house.

"Pálinka?" she asked, well accustomed by now to my emergency visits.

"I definitely need one, but I can't. I'm on my way to Pienza for lunch." I handed her my phone. "Read this. I think I'm going crazy."

Raffaella read the email and then looked through the attachment. "So where's the money?"

"These nitwits sent it to the wrong account. But I guess after ten months of not having been paid, it's laudable that somebody is at last *trying* to pay me."

"Not trying hard enough, though. Whose account might it be?"

"I think I know." I scrolled through my sent emails. "Here it is!" I showed Raffaella an email that I had sent Pio in April that listed Lesley's and my bank details. Both account numbers were neatly written next to our names, one below the other. "Whoever made the payment must have swapped the two."

"*Mamma mia*, do they ever get anything right?"

"Sometimes. At least that's what people keep telling me. Anyway, the good news is that the money has been sent to Lesley's account by mistake. Don Vito's charity owes her even more than me, and she really needs to be paid more urgently than anybody else."

My phone beeped again.

"Another email from Pio."

"Ah, good," Raffaella said. "He must have realized that he got this totally wrong."

"It doesn't look like it. 'Meier' is the only word written in the subject line."

"Wow!" Raffaella looked at the email. "Looks like a WANTED notice!"

Skipping the salutation again, like in his first email of the morning—after all, infidels like me no longer deserved to be addressed by their first name, let alone by a friendly *Cara* or *Ciao*—Pio cut straight to the core of the matter. Attached to the email were two documents that I was supposed to open and sign. The first consisted of the contract I had been waiting for since April (hallelujah!); the second was a resignation letter that stated that I had decided to quit working for the charity for personal reasons. My full name, including my Swiss middle name, had already been inserted into the resignation letter, and all of it had been spelled immaculately—a feat that not even Sergio and my own children managed to pull off all the time.

"You have to give it to them," Raffaella said, "they screw up a lot, but when they decide to get rid of somebody, they make a real effort to get everything right."

In fact, as I could see farther down in Pio's email, the resignation letter had been prepared by the charity's legal consultant earlier that morning. Even though the supreme head of the charity was extremely busy, he had evidently managed to find the time to discuss my case with several people. Sadly, none of them had been me.

"Sure you don't want a coffee at least?" Raffaella asked.

"I'd love one, but I'm already running late." I got back into the car.

"You know the thing I don't get?" Raffaella was standing next to the Dacia.

"What?" I asked through the window.

"Take an Italian and a Swiss and imagine that they are discussing the best way to prepare a pasta sauce—let's say spaghetti carbonara, or even just a straightforward tomato sauce—which of the two would you believe?"

"The Italian," I said, even though I couldn't quite see where she was going with this.

"Exactly! Now take the same two people again. The Italian vows solemnly that he made a bank transfer, and the Swiss insists that it hasn't arrived yet..."

It had been a miserable morning, but I couldn't help but laugh.

"You'd believe the Swiss, wouldn't you? In fact, forget about all that cheese, chocolate and snow-topped mountain peaks, because who, if not you guys, would know how to check a bank account? Tell me, *who*? And this is what any Italian employer with a bit of self-awareness should know. But what does this Pio guy do? Impersonating our country's worst stereotype, instigated by the complaints of his coworker in the role of holy Mary, he goes off like an H-bomb. Takes everything personally. Feels attacked and offended. Unduly criticized. And sure that this is a question of honor and dignity and that the—not yet hired—employee needs to be taught a lesson, he storms off to call in the legal team..." Raffaella bent down to pull out a weed. She threw it over the embankment leading down to the wood and shook her head. "And to think that all he needed to do was spend five calm minutes at his desk to check a few emails and figure out what had gone wrong with his bank transfer."

I turned on the engine, but Raffaella wanted to add one more thing.

"And you know what's even worse?" I had lived in Italy long enough to know what she was about to say. "Our politicians function the same way."

***

I met Pio and his team one more time in the charity's office in the city. Pio, probably worried about repercussions from the prefecture or a worker's union I might talk to, tried to convince me in every possible way to sign the copies of the contract and resignation letter that they had printed out for me. I declined and left.

Sergio had taken the day off and was waiting for me in the car. For moral support? I had asked him. To celebrate, he had corrected.

It was the first warm day of summer and we drove to the sea for a day at the beach. Sergio turned the stereo on and I recognized the singer's voice after a few beats.

"Hotel Rif?" I asked.

"Yep! Since you missed the concert."

We got off the highway and drove through the countryside. Crimson poppies fringed green fields and hundred-year-old stone pine trees lined the roads. I was just settling into my newfound worry-free lifestyle when Sergio slowed the car. A tall girl was standing next to the road. *Hope*, I thought for a moment, but it wasn't her. Two more girls were waiting for clients in a clearing a bit farther on. We didn't recognize either of them.

"Still hoping to save them?" Sergio asked.

"No, I'll leave the saving of souls to the religious crowd. But there must be a better way than looking away and pretending sex workers don't exist."

Sergio drove down a narrow sandy road and parked the car in the shade of an umbrella pine tree near the beach. We walked along the shore to a small bar to buy sandwiches and a bottle of white wine. Sitting in the sand, I watched the sea and enjoyed the calm. This was what I had moved to Italy for. This view. A beautiful beach with nobody around. And a good glass of wine from time to time.

I fell asleep and woke up to the sound of a fishing boat chugging through the waves. I watched its slow trajectory on the deep blue sea. Sergio stood in the water, waving for me to come in. "As long as it lasts," he shouted, pointing to the sky. Dark clouds had formed; the weather was about to change.

Contemplating the first swim of the season, with my feet in the cold water, I looked at the Mediterranean Sea and thought of Odysseus, and of all the people who keep risking passage on these treacherous waters. And how, in defiance of the gods, just like the Greek hero before them, they keep holding on for dear life—to rubber dinghies and battered fishing boats—in the hope of finding a better one on the other side.

Afterword

Don Vito's charity eventually paid me seven months after I stopped working in Dogana. It took another seven months to convince the board to finally pay Lesley too. Teresa is now the vice-mayor of the village where she started her political career. She never talked to me about what went wrong with the charity. I asked her several times and told her to call me if she wanted me to include her views in this book. She never did.

Joyce, Precious, Hope, Izogie and Fola waited nearly a year for their hearings with the human rights commission in Florence. All of their asylum requests were denied. They have all lodged appeals against the commission's decisions. All of their first appeals have been rejected, and two and a half years after arriving in Italy, they now wait for the court hearing for their second appeals. Rita, who arrived in Sicily several months before the other girls, has already received the results from her second appeal and has been granted the right to stay in Italy under humanitarian protection for the next three years.

Joyce lives in Rome and told me during our last phone call that she still works as a babysitter. Precious, Izogie and Rita were transferred to a different refugee home shortly after I stopped working in Dogana. Precious and Izogie still live there. Rita has moved out and is living in Bologna, where she says she sometimes works as a cleaner. The last time I talked to Joyce, she said she still lived with the family in Rome and worked as their babysitter. Fola lives in Genoa, where she works with a friend whom she helps sell things. She laughed when I asked her what exactly it is they sell. It is always nice to hear from them, and it is as it always has been—I am not the person they'd ever tell what's really going on. Maybe Hope would have one day, but I haven't been able to contact her. Her phone number is no longer in use and her Facebook account has been deleted. The other girls have not heard from her in a long time. I hope she is okay, wherever she is.

Don Vito's charity keeps running several refugee homes. The one in Dogana has become a home for young men from Western Africa, Pakistan and Bangladesh, and things seem to work out better now. The women's shelter in the countryside is presently mostly used for refugees. Domestic violence is as much of a problem as ever, but with the current situation, financial support is more streamlined and easier to obtain for running refugee homes than women's shelters (various women's shelters have closed in Italy during recent years because of lack of funding).

Nour and her daughters, Farah and Leila, live in a social housing project in Berlin. Nour suffers from a lot of backache. Supporting her disabled daughter during the long and difficult journey took its toll. Farah has already reached level four of the six-level certification of the Goethe institute, but although she is doing extremely well with her language classes (we now only text and talk in German), she is worried because she hasn't found a job yet. The three of them live in an apartment on the top floor but are hoping to find a different setup to make Leila's life easier.

Ida had a rough first year in Germany. She couldn't stay permanently with her cousin (who shares a one-room apartment with her husband) and has stayed in a few refugee homes. She started a literacy and German class towards the end of her first year but hardly attended the lessons because of bouts of depression and recurring physical problems. She met a young man from Gambia in a refugee home she moved to in her second year. The couple is now expecting a baby and Ida sounds more hopeful. She is still waiting for the outcome of her asylum request.

Aziz and his Gambian friends all received negative verdicts from the commission. The refugee home in our village has closed, and they were moved to a new one in an even more remote location in the Tuscan outback. The court hearing dates for Aziz's first appeal have been set for two and a half years after his first arrival in Italy. Discouraged and tired from the long wait, two of Aziz's young friends packed their bags and crossed the borders to France and Germany.

Lesley and Vera have moved to a small apartment in the Tuscan countryside. Lesley's court case is stalling, and she still can't see her children for more than an hour every week. To this day, Vera has still not been allowed to visit her grandchildren in the children's home where they have been living for the last three years. On the website for this book, www.acrossthebigbluesea.com, there is an option to donate funds to hire an expert lawyer for Lesley and Vera, which is the only way to make sure their case isn't lost forever in Italy's biased and maddeningly slow legal system.

Switzerland has so far repaid $723 million of the alleged $2.2 billion that Nigerian dictator Sani Abacha looted and stashed in European bank accounts during his reign in the nineties. An agreement between the Swiss and Nigerian governments states that at least another $321 million will be returned to Nigeria.

Acknowledgments

A big thank you to family and friends for being patient and supportive during the time I took to write this book. *Un grazie di cuore* to Maggie O'Riordan, Pia Ghosh Roy and Ursula Reuter-Mayring, the steadfast and encouraging first readers of this manuscript. Many more friends have helped with good advice during my time in Dogana—you know who you are (or you'll find out once our olive oil is delivered to your doorstep).

Lesley, Vera, Hope, Joyce, Rita, Izogie, Ida, Farah, Nour and Aziz knew that I was writing this book and approved of it, even though all I could do was tell the story from my point of view, which leaves out information and episodes that they might have included or told in a different way.

Thank you to Jørgen Carling for his permission to quote at length from his informative article "Trafficking in Women from Nigeria to Europe," which was published in 2005 on the Migration Policy Institute website.

For resources and further reading, please consult www.across-thebigbluesea.com, where you'll find links to articles, books and documentaries about sex work, migration and human trafficking that I consulted and keep consulting. I started out wondering whether abolition—as in the oft-cited Swedish model—could be the solution to these problems. But during my time in Dogana, I came to believe that not repression but decriminalization is the best way forward to improve the lives, health and legal standing of sex workers (which is the case in

New Zealand, for example). Bringing the sex industry into the daylight will also make it easier to find and help women who have been trafficked without punishing the sex workers who have chosen this profession deliberately. Sex workers—united by a growing number of professional organizations all over the world—are the first ones to ask for recognition, labor rights and an end to discrimination, so please listen to their voices first to develop an informed opinion, or before voting in this matter.

For in-depth resources, a playlist with the book's soundtrack and photos of the view from our Tuscan olive grove, visit:

WWW.ACROSSTHEBIGBLUESEA.COM